MW00817857

NATURAL ESP

△   △   △

The ESP Core and Its Raw Characteristics

INGO SWANN

AN ELEANOR FRIEDE BOOK

BANTAM BOOKS

TORONTO · NEW YORK · LONDON · SYDNEY · AUCKLAND

For permission to quote allied and similar issues within the content of this present book, I must acknowledge and express my thanks to:

Excerpts from THE ESP EXPERIENCE: A Psychiatric Validation by Jan Ehrenwald, M.D. Copyright © 1978 by Basic Books, Inc., Publishers. Reprinted by permission of the publisher.

Excerpt from THE MANIPULATION OF HUMAN BEHAVIOUR, edited by Biderman and Zimmer from an article by L. E. Hinkle, Jr.: "The physiological state of the interrogation subject as it affects brain function." John Wiley & Sons, Inc., N.Y., 1961.

Excerpt from ENCYCLOPEDIA OF OCCULTISM AND PARAPSYCHOLOGY, edited by Leslie Shepard. Copyright © 1984 by Gale Research Company; reprinted by permission of the publisher, Gale Research, 1984.

Excerpt from FORBIDDEN UNIVERSE by Leo Talamonti reprinted with permission of Stein and Day Publishers and Garnstone Press Ltd. Copyright © 1974 by Leo Talamonti.

Excerpt from PARAPSYCHOLOGY AND CONTEMPORARY SCIENCE reprinted with permission of Plenum Publishing Corporation.

Excerpt from A NEW SCIENCE OF LIFE by Rupert Sheldrake reprinted by permission of Jeremy P. Tarcher, Inc. and Muller, Blond & White, Ltd. Copyright © 1981, 1985 by Rupert Sheldrake.

Excerpt from PRECONSCIOUSNESS PROCESSING by Norman Dixon by permission of the author.

Excerpts from SCIENCE AND PARASCIENCE by Brian Inglis reprinted by kind permission of Curtis Brown and Hodder & Stoughton Limited on behalf of the author. Copyright © 1984 Brian Inglis.

Excerpts from MENTAL RADIO by Upton Sinclair reprinted with permission of David Sinclair.

Excerpts from MIND TO MIND by René Warcollier. Copyright 1948 by Creative Age Press. Copyright renewed © 1975 by Farrar Straus & Giroux, Inc.

Excerpts reprinted by permission from Ernest Taves, "M. Warcollier's Investigations in Telepathy." *Journal of the American Society for Psychical Research*, 1939 (Dec.), 33, 356–369.

Drawings excerpted from the SRI International experiments: Private publications.

Excerpt from ART AND VISUAL PERCEPTION by Rudolf Arnheim reprinted by permission of University of California Press.

Excerpt from DRAWING ON THE ARTIST WITHIN by Betty Edwards reprinted by permission of Simon & Schuster, Inc. Copyright © 1986 by Betty Edwards.

Excerpt from *New Art Examiner*, "Changing Paradigms" by Suzi Gablick, June 1985.

Excerpt from THE COSMIC WEB by N. Katherine Hayles. Reprinted by permission of Cornell University Press.

NATURAL ESP
A Bantam Book / July 1987

New Age and the accompanying figure design as well as the statement "the search for meaning, growth and change" are trademarks of Bantam Books, Inc.

All rights reserved.
Copyright © 1987 by Psychic Alternatives, Inc.
Cover art copyright © 1987 by Gabriel Molano.
Book design by Kingsley Parker.
This book may not be reproduced in whole or in part, by mimeograph or any other means, without permission.
For information address: Bantam Books, Inc.

Library of Congress Cataloging-in-Publication Data

Swann, Ingo, 1933–
  Natural ESP.

  "Bantam new age books"—Prelim. p.
  Bibliography: p.
  1. Extrasensory perception. I. Title.
BF1321.S92 1987   133.8   86-47897
ISBN 0-553-34417-X

Published simultaneously in the United States and Canada

Bantam Books are published by Bantam Books, Inc. Its trademark, consisting of the words "Bantam Books" and the portrayal of a rooster, is Registered in U.S. Patent and Trademark Office and in other countries. Marca Registrada. Bantam Books, Inc., 666 Fifth Avenue, New York, New York 10103.

PRINTED IN THE UNITED STATES OF AMERICA

O   0 9 8 7 6 5 4 3 2

To Harold E. Puthoff
for his courage

△ ACKNOWLEDGMENTS △

It has been an honor and a pleasure during the past sixteen years to work among several hundred pioneering souls in the combined fields of psychical research, parapsychology, and psychoenergetics, and each of them deserves my deepest thanks. I am especially grateful to a large group of interested people who have brought both substance and direction to the long and painful hours of research and experimentation, but who would prefer not to be mentioned for professional reasons.

In addition to all the above, the management of SRI International is due special thanks for their long and continued support of a research effort that has frequently come under attack by detractors, and to the numerous staff of the Psychoenergetics Project there. Specific thanks must go to Dr. Harold E. Puthoff, to whom this present book is dedicated, for his staunch support and his ability to endure through hardships, and to Dr. Edwin C. May, Dr. Charles Tart, and to Martha Tompson whose research assistance has been invaluable: and Russell Targ, Hella Hammid, Keith Harrary, and Gary Langford, whose work in analogous problems of ESP has made life more exciting.

I have always been indebted to the early support of the Board of Trustees of the American Society for Psychical Research, and to Dr. Karlis Osis, Dr. Janet Mitchell, and Mrs. Laura F. Knipe; to Dr. Arthur J. Ellison of the University of London and long-time president of the Society for Psychical Research; and to the Parapsychology Foundation and its tremendous library, especially to Mr. Wayne Norman who has helped locate obscure but valuable sources. Creative support has always been forthcoming from Dr. Jan Ehrenwald, Dr. Gertrude R. Schmeidler, Dr. Jacques Vallee, Dr. William A. Tiller, Mr. Trammell Crow, and Mr. Martin Ebon, among many others.

The editorial horrors of making the complex issues talked about in this book more easily accessible have been eased by the professional insights of Eleanor Friede and Barbara Bowen. I am also indebted to Tom Joyce, who has provided the finished original art work, and to Julia Turchuk, who helped organize the many picture-drawings in this book.

Last, but far from the least, the most profound debt of gratitude must go to my "guinea pig" predecessors who found the courage to bring their fragile talents into the clinical laboratory setting and before an unbelieving world, and upon whose cumulative work the context of this present book has been made possible.

△ CONTENTS △

NATURAL ESP

△　　　△　　　△

△ FOREWORD △

Few topics are as controversial as the existence of ESP—
and for so little reason. Not only has this faculty been demonstrated in hundreds of careful experiments by reputable
researchers; it is experienced with increasing regularity by
most people. We call it "hits," hunches, gut feelings,
creative inspiration; we even joke about it, but we would
be ashamed to say we use and enjoy it. This despite
several decades of polls and surveys indicating that most
of us have had "extrasensory" experiences and believe in
them . . . and that the better-educated are even more
convinced that the phenomenon is real.

Our failure as a society to acknowledge this fundamental
ability may be a mark of our general reticence in mapping
inner realities: dreams, imagery, memory, thoughts, feelings, the creative process itself. It's as if half of life is
relegated to second-class status. Habitual patterns of communication make our collective life a facade of a facade.

We speak to each other, but we seldom voice the deeper
thoughts behind our speech. We ask "How are you?" as if
we could not see and sense the well- or ill-being of the
other. We remark on or envy the charisma of some people, without wondering about the nature of their radiant
energy; it is as if a vital mode of communication, the use of
our inner senses, were nonexistent or a mere trick.

In the years I have studied the phenomenon of high
creativity, I have been struck by the naturalness with

which visionary people use their unexplained perceptual abilities. Creatively successful people, whether artists or entrepreneurs, readily acknowledge the importance of hunches and inner "guidance." In a recent survey of the chief executives of the fastest-growing companies, all named the same "greatest regret" of their career: the occasions when they failed to heed their intuition.

In this book, Ingo Swann has made yet another contribution to our collective good. The gifted artist who helped pioneer the methodology for "remote viewing" research now offers a simple and freeing perspective on ESP. It is real, it is natural, and you can readily discover it in yourself. You can even repeat and refine your experiments.

His writing style is characterized by the same gentle, nonjudgmental approach essential to reliable ESP. He points out, explains, describes; he doesn't preach.

It is rare for an artist to know, let alone reveal, his creative process. It is even rarer for a gifted psychic to demystify his specialty. In *Natural ESP,* Ingo Swann does both. Besides showing us the strategies for "picture drawings," he also reveals the scientific, analytical side of the creative mind as he sets out the historic case for mind-to-mind communication.

Whether the reader is convinced that ESP is natural or is merely curious, this wise and useful book will engage the mind with fresh, exciting possibilities.

Marilyn Ferguson
Los Angeles
June 1986

△ PREFACE △

This book describes certain important newly discovered elements of extrasensory perception which have never before appeared in the general parapsychological literature. The concept that a natural ESP "core" exists in all of us as a general *and* individualized human talent is the product of my research and efforts to develop my own ESP potential. I was able to locate my ESP core only after I noticed certain basic similar characteristics in the work of psychic subjects who had preceded me. These similar characteristics had never been commented upon, and to a large degree, it seems as if they have been ignored.

By categorizing these similar elements, I was eventually able to see that my own ESP was working (or trying to work) along lines that were almost identical to those of my predecessors. I made my first "discovery" in 1971 by going back into the research literature, right to its beginning in 1882. After 1971, I was able to observe that when other people, none of them trained psychics, tried an ESP experience, they also showed results that bore similarities to my attempts and to those of the earlier subjects.

The similarities among the historical examples (many of which are given in this book) not only help reveal the nature of the raw ESP core, but also finally establish beyond any doubt that extrasensory perception exists as a rudimentary talent—a potentially powerful one among the list of other human natural talents.

Understanding these communally shared ESP elements will be immeasurably helpful to those who want to locate and begin developing their own extrasensory perceptions. It will also be meaningful to those seeking a better understanding of general ESP, its high points and its problems.

The idea that extrasensory abilities are going to take on enormous importance in the near future is not just another empty prediction. The world's three most important powers—the Soviet Union, the United States, and the People's Republic of China—have mounted increasingly large programs to research extrasensory potentials. Though each of these powers is cloaking its investigations into ESP in secrecy, an imposing amount of smoke has begun rising. It is dark smoke, and terms such as the "ESP threat" or "achieving an ESP advantage" are becoming common parlance. These terms suggest the nature of the fires smoldering beneath the smoke of secrecy.

For it to have a more positive influence on our future, ESP must be found useful at the grass roots level where goal-oriented individuals can perceive its forms and applications for the common good. Only those individuals who have made some effort to locate and understand ESP as a personal experience will be in a position to comprehend more fully the potential of ESP. They are the advanced thinkers who will redefine the boundaries of consciousness and provide the foundation for the new age of applied ESP.

Ingo Swann

△ INTRODUCTION △

This is a book about ESP. But it is not the usual book about ESP. It is not another attempt to convince the world that ESP exists, nor to proclaim the author's talent, nor to chronicle the author's vicissitudes encountered during more than a decade of activity as a volunteer subject in a half-dozen major ESP laboratories across the United States. Rather, it is a book wherein the hero of the story is the ESP process itself and what it seems to be telling us about the human state.

Swann's goal in authoring this book is nothing less than to guide the reader into experiencing for himself or herself a personal contact with what Swann has dubbed the "ESP core," hypothesized to exist in us all, proponent and skeptic alike. In short, this how-to book marks a pathway for the reader to follow in order to discover at a personal level the apparent universal capacity of the human mind to transcend the usual barriers of space and time. Taking this approach, Swann rises above the continued "quibbling" about whether or not someone else has managed to cheat in an ESP experiment.

Swann is uniquely qualified to be the pathfinder for such a journey. He has been intimately involved in the broad-scale resurgence of interest in ESP that has characterized the last decade and a half. Beginning with his first timorous efforts as a volunteer subject for experiments in out-of-body perception at the American Society for Psychi-

cal Research in the summer of 1971, Swann has chosen
the difficult road of laboratory experimentation. With this
choice each step is taken in the glare of the spotlight of
statistical evaluation and alternative hypotheses, a glare
too harsh for most who would explore their ESP potential.
Participating in further efforts with Professor Gertrude
Schmeidler in the Psychology Department at the City
College of New York, and with the remote viewing pro-
gram at SRI International, among others, Swann soon
found his role expanding beyond that of simple test subject to that of innovative pioneer and researcher, providing creative insight into the very foundations of the ESP
process itself.

Perhaps contrary to expectation in a book on fostering
ESP experience, Swann's first step is to focus on what is
wrong with ESP, why it frustrates the expectations of the
novice and the experienced alike. Sometimes charming,
sometimes acerbic, Swann's probing of the myths surrounding ESP unearths a major fault lying across the camps of
the proponents and skeptics alike; rather than being true
to the data, to what can actually be observed, both proponent and skeptic attempt to force ESP to meet their own
preconceived notions as to how it *ought* to exhibit itself.

Proponents tend to focus on those rare instances in
which an ESP result mimics ordinary sensory experience
in its clarity of verbal description or visual presentation;
skeptics tend to focus on the lack of such clarity in the
preponderence of the data. Swann undercuts both approaches
in a diligent effort to ferret out the significance of what
actually takes place during a typical attempt at ESP contact with a remote target, from which emerges a typical
response that is typically ambiguous. Indeed, Swann's contribution to the field as a researcher is highlighted by his
ceaseless effort to explore and understand these ambigu-
ities; when, where, and how they occur, and how one
could be trained to use each facet of the subjective ESP
experience to enhance objective performance.

This book begins the journey with some of the earliest published work in the field (circa 1880s), and ends with laboratory research ongoing at the present time. Surprising mileposts emerge along the way: the periodic turning away from certain classes of experiments that are more productive and reliable than others, the apparent degradation of performance that can be induced by the simple act of (mis)labeling the various facets of the phenomena under study, and a perverse (unconscious?) tendency for experimental ESP protocols to be developed in directions that increase the mismatch with regard to the laws that appear to govern such functioning. Swann's commitment is to a reversal of these trends, with a concomitant reemergence of higher levels of ESP functioning.

Careful examination of the data indicates that even in nonstellar ESP performance there is often, first, evidence for contact with the target and, furthermore, discernible patterns in the types of errors that have insinuated themselves into the process to degrade the result. Drawing from the experiences of himself and others, Swann's analysis of this situation leads him to the conclusion that the major problem in ESP lies not in an engineering concept of the transmission of a signal from there to here, but in the internal processing that takes place here. (As Shakespeare's Cassius says in *Julius Caesar*, "The fault, dear Brutus, is not in our stars, but in ourselves.") It would appear that an ESP signal must run a veritable gauntlet on its way from the "ESP core" to frontal verbal consciousness, with every possible opportunity for derailment along the way by preconceptions, premature attempts at labeling, and internal editing. This key recognition leads Swann to a specific model of the ESP process, a model that introduces such concepts as a "deeper self" connected to a "second reality."

Most importantly, the model that has emerged predicts that strategies that undercut verbalization and imaging in favor of a more primal kinesthetic response (involving hieroglyphic-like sketching, almost doodling) constitute the royal road from primary ESP contact to recognizable result. This is in stark contrast to a century of academic research into ESP (begun by the founding of the British Society for Psychic Research in 1882) that has seen a trend toward more verbal-oriented, decision-making (guessing) ESP procedures, strategies that involve functions residing high in the nervous system. Compared to this tradition, the approach described herein, simple but not simplistic, apparently contrary to historical trend and expectation, calls for a return to a response pattern more akin perhaps to the gut-level intuition of naturally occurring ESP than to the sanitized button presses of our high-tech laboratories. This concept, buttressed by examples separated by dozens of years, thousands of miles, and generations of outlook, would seem to lie behind some of the more striking examples produced in the sketch-oriented remote viewing studies at SRI International (in which Swann has played a major role), Princeton University, the Mind Science Foundation of San Antonio, and the Mobius Society in Los Angeles, or in the earlier work of Upton Sinclair as reported in *Mental Radio*.

Having worked with Swann over a number of years to develop effective remote viewing protocols, I am not surprised that if a new path through the potential pitfalls could lead to better functioning, Swann would be among those to find it (or rediscover it) in our time, and recognize its significance. Never one to follow fads, and always one to hold a position if he thought it was important for the development of better ESP functioning, he kept before his inner eye two basic tenets: (1) ESP is a naturally occurring phenomenon basic to all humankind, and thus it is the functioning and *not* the person (including himself) that should be of primary importance in this study; (2) with a disciplined observational approach it should be possible to develop techniques capable of eliciting ESP with a quality approaching the startling clarity that sometimes occurs spontaneously in life.

Combining rare talents for subjective experience and objective critique, internal analysis and external research, Swann presents here his status report with the hope that it will not only lead the reader into a greater appreciation of his or her own capacity for ESP, but also permit a personal glimpse into the deeper implications for humankind as a whole.

Harold E. Puthoff, Ph.D.
Institute for Advanced Studies
    at Austin
Austin, Texas

△ ONE △

A New Stage
for ESP

*The question is whether parapsychology, having suc-
ceeded in "breeding" a new, properly refined, do-
mesticated, and mathematically treatable species of
forced-choice psi [ESP] phenomena, is not apt to lose
sight of their original prototype, a more elusive but
culturally and biologically more significant one.**

I think we can all agree on one thing: Every
system has bugs. Bugs—those invisible critters—
are what cause a system to break down. If something has
too many bugs, it won't work at all.

If you try to make a bugged-up system work, you will
probably end up pulling your hair out and gnashing your
teeth. What is needed is a debugger. It's actually a very
venerable but little acknowledged profession. The smart
debugger keeps behind the scenes because he knows that
any system designed by the high-powered brains of man
cannot admit to having bugs. That would make the brain
less than glorious, a state none of us likes to focus on for

---

*Jan Ehrenwald, *The ESP Experience*, Basic Books, New York, 1978, p. 11.

1

too long. So debuggers work to discover unexpected defects, faults, flaws, or imperfections. Then, the system starts working again. Often it is a new system altogether.

Dr. Jan Ehrenwald, a parapsychologist and scholar who has spent a lifetime studying the intricacies of ESP, has described parapsychology as:

> a systematic inquiry into such out-of-the-ordinary occurrences as telepathy, clairvoyance, psychokinesis, and precognition which, until recently, have largely remained outside the pale of science. Parapsychology, therefore, is supposed to represent a new frontier of psychology, seeking to advance man's knowledge of himself into unknown territory. Yet parapsychology does not break entirely new ground. . . .*

Parapsychology (and its predecessor, psychical research) has been around for a little over a hundred years. Psychic abilities have been hunted madly during this time—alas, to little avail. While the mathematical system taken altogether shows that ESP *does* exist, none of ESP's larger, more productive issues have come to light. Its basic components are still elusive. After a hundred years of seeking, parapsychologists are embarrassed, while skeptics are jubilant.

It is a strange situation. We all know, personally, that extrasensory perception does exist. Spontaneous ESP keeps happening, on a rather large scale, but parapsychologists just can't get a handle on it. At the same time, parapsychology frequently harvests rigorous resistance from sources outside itself. This is understandable if you realize that parapsychology and what it represents constitutes the bugs in several other science systems that have been designed

*Ibid., p. 3.

without including the realities of ESP and psi.* People cling to *their* systems. Many antipsychic authorities have admitted publicly that if psychic things are proved true, then *their* systems will be wrong. So we can see where the resistance comes from.

But does this explain parapsychology's general lack of progress? Parapsychologists themselves admit unofficially that progress seems to be dragging its feet. Few and far between are those who will *officially proclaim* the total existence of any particular psychic phenomenon. They insist they are still *studying* them. It doesn't take much to understand that the lack of proclamation corresponds to the lack of trenchant discovery. Now, after a hundred years of diligent effort, the time is drawing near when parapsychology will have to start looking for the bugs in the very systems it is employing to track down the paranormal.

Extrasensory perception is like the enormous shifting-dunes of sand in a desert, always changing, soft, and fluid. Perhaps it will be seen that parapsychology has been trying to negotiate these dunes with horses, whose sharp hooves sink into the sand, when all along they should have been riding camels, whose big soft foot pads are perfect for desert travel.

This analogy helps us grasp the fundamental issue that continues to hang over a progressive future development of extrasensory perception as a reality within ourselves. It also helps us comprehend Dr. Ehrenwald's penetrating insight when he says:

> The question is, to what extent can the experimental evidence be regarded as a duplication in

---

*Psi is a Greek letter used by parapsychologists to embrace all unusual mental phenomena such as telepathy, clairvoyance, precognition, and unusual physical phenomena such as psychokinesis (movement of objects without physical contact). It was first used as an acronym to replace the word "psychic" which was scientifically unpopular, but in the 1950s came to be accepted as a word in itself.

> the laboratory of ESP phenomena as they are encountered spontaneously, "in the raw," under conditions of ordinary life. . . . We have to ask whether . . . cultivating the "small fry" that can be observed in the ESP laboratory, does not run the risk of losing sight of the "big game" of major psi occurrences of the type which have struck man's mind with wonder and awe from the dawn of history? It may be that by opening our door by little more than a tiny crack, we bar the entrance into our purview of all but a few flattened out microscopic slices off a lost psychic reality.*

New facts and ideas are often alien to the way we are used to thinking about things. Any author presenting something new is obliged to set a stage that uses familiar references to help illuminate the unfamiliar.

When it comes to extrasensory perception, setting the stage is difficult for two reasons that are important.

ESP Is Elusive

The phenomena we label "extrasensory" are not very well understood even after a hundred years of researching them. There are few normal standards that can be used to help.

Parapsychology has given sufficient clinical testing to the phenomena so that it is practically impossible to deny they exist. The proof is actually quite colossal. But the mechanisms that cause ESP to function have remained invisible and elusive so that there is only mini-

*Ibid., p. 11.

mal contact with what actually underlies the various ESP phenomena.

An additional difficulty is that ESP cannot be studied objectively—that is, as something outside ourselves. It arises from places in our overall mental makeup that are not visible to our normal consciousness. It surfaces in ways that are not logical compared to the usual ways we interpret things.

Extrasensory events do not concretize themselves very well, at least under the methods of exploration that have been used so far. They fade in and out of our awarenesses and minds leaving little behind as tangible evidence that they were even there. This often leaves even the most devoted believers in ESP with the futile feeling that they are chasing shadows that are constantly moving, with nothing that can be seen to cast the shadows in the first place. As a result, extrasensory perception has never achieved a normalized status—even *within* parapsychology, the science that studies the phenomena.

ESP Is Covered with "Labels" That May Be False

If the invisible and intangible nature of ESP is not enough to cause continual confusion, the terms we use to describe these invisibles *have* become set in cement.

The terms "extrasensory perception (ESP)," "telepathy," "clairvoyance," "precognition" and so forth have long been common concepts and household words, even though no one really knows for sure exactly what they stand for.

Using the word "telepathy" as an example, we can get some idea of the problems involved.

Telepathy is variously defined as direct mind-to-mind

communication, or communication from one mind to another through other than normal sensory channels.

Something like what is implied by these definitions might indeed eventually turn out to be true. But right now there is absolutely no evidence at all to support those definitions.

The best that can be said is there are instances in which two or more minds seem to be in some kind of rapport with each other, in which what is in one mind can appear in the other's. It is only an assumption that one mind is "sending" directly to another mind, which is "receiving." Yet terms and definitions like this one have been accepted as valid conceptions when, in reality, they are only labels that represent something we think *might* exist. In other words, something that is invisible and whose basic elements are totally unknown has been given a label to describe it *as if it truly exists*.

It is worthwhile digging into the word "telepathy" to demonstrate how it became the label it did. When the word was coined in 1882 by F.W.H. Myers, the basic idea was to link up distance (tele-) with empathy—telepathy. It was meant as a name for an apparent fact—"a coincidence between two persons' thoughts which requires a causal explanation"—and it was defined as a "transmission of thought independent of the recognized channels of sense." Myers presupposed that the term involved no attempt at explanation, yet it was soon construed as such.

A decade before, electromagnetic radiation had been discovered, and soon radioactive emissions were confirmed. Telepathy collected around it the concepts of radiations and emissions. It was assumed that a mind could also radiate and emit, and the something radiated or emitted was being "sent" across a distance, where it was received, like a radio, by another mind. The invisible-unknown elements of telepathy were compared to and modeled after radiations and emissions. The comparison was accepted for, after all, it seemed to fit.

It is now known that telepathy can take place in environments impervious to all known forms of radiation or emissions, so the radiation-sending theory is a bust. Yet we continue to think of telepathy as if we know it *works* that way. As long as our concepts are trapped in that special label, we are unlikely to think of telepathy in any other way.

Our concepts (and consequently our heads) are glued together with many labels of this kind which refer only to things we think we know. All this label glue can be referred to as the "representational universe." As long as we continue to think of things as we have only chanced to represent them to ourselves, the real facts of the unknown will remain invisible and unrecognized.

All psychic phenomena are cloaked with labels such as this, and parapsychology struggles valiantly within them.

Fitting New Facts and Ideas into Old Labels

The question immediately arises: Can new facts and ideas about ESP fit into its old labels? The reason for considering this question at all is that labels, once accepted in dictionaries and as household words, continue to have power over the ways we think about them.

This question has incredible importance upon what is to follow in the rest of this book. For example, in 1971 when I first volunteered as a psychic test subject, I tried to evoke my telepathy, clairvoyance, and out-of-body perceptions through the labels as I (then) conceived them. The results were negative and emotionally quite humiliating.

Based upon these first results, the only possible and logical conclusion would have been that I did not possess

ESP at all, and that would have been the end of it. Yet I could not believe that, since there were many cases of ESP frequently demonstrated. Contrasting these early failures were events in my life that seemed to me obviously extrasensory in nature. So what was wrong?

If you read a few basic books on what is known about how the mind functions (which I immediately did), the results can be very illuminating. As Lawrence Hinkle, Jr., has pointed out:

> The brain, the organ that deals with information, also organizes its responses on the basis of information previously fed into it. This information, in the form of a personality developed through the experience of a lifetime, as well as immediate attitudes and the awareness of the immediate situation, conditions the way the brain will react to a given situation.*

As I considered this insight, it gradually became clear that spontaneous ESP events (which I had experienced often, and which most other people do also) were something quite different from the way my intellectual learning was thinking about them.

Spontaneous ESP events occurred by themselves via rules and logic of their own (usually taking normal intellectual consciousness by surprise). But when I tried to evoke an ESP event by using my intellectual understanding of ESP as a basis (the information previously fed in), nothing happened. Using the word "telepathy" did not trigger mind-to-mind contact nor did using the word "clairvoyance" trigger much clairvoyance, nor did trying to move intellectually into an "altered state" provide

*L. E. Hinkle, Jr., in "The physiological state of the interrogation subject as it affects brain function," in *The Manipulation of Human Behaviour*, Albert B. Biderman and Herbert Zimmer (eds.), John Wiley & Sons, New York, 1961, pp. 33–34.

much help. (After all, *which* altered state should one move into?)

I was able to conclude (correctly so) that ESP must work and function on its own by mechanisms not recognizable to my brain learning, even though I possessed lots of labels that served me intellectually. There was no direct connection between these labels and real ESP mechanisms. To put this another way, my labels served as filters or barriers to true real ESP experience! The labels were acting as mental preconceptions about what *should be* experienced intellectually, when in reality (as it turned out) these preconceptions were the night side to ESP's day-side mechanisms. It was only after I learned to detach myself from the power of these labels that some of ESP's mechanisms revealed themselves.

In answer to the question as to whether or not new facts and ideas about extrasensory perception can be fit into its old labels, my supposition (based on sixteen years of in-depth experience) is that this fitting will be minimal. We have to prepare ourselves to view the actual mechanisms of ESP quite independent of the old labels, if for no other reason than they have not proved themselves after one hundred years.

The Major Backdrop of the New Stage—People Are Not the Dumb Animals They Are Often Thought to Be

All the above considered, setting a new stage on which to consider extrasensory perception is not an enviable task. On one hand we have the invisible unknowns. On the other, we have ingrained and accepted labels that allow us intellectually to think we know what we are dealing with, but actually do not.

In this book, I want to introduce a number of concepts such as "mind mound," "mind manifesting," "the ESP core," and "penetrating the ESP core," all of which will describe elements of extrasensory perception in a new way. But none of these concepts can effectively be understood unless we go beneath the already-existing labels and find a new cutting edge for a novel comprehension of how the extrasensory processes are actually working.

In casting about for where this cutting edge might lay, I've decided to appeal to the generally shared human attribute for experiencing.

I'm of the opinion that people are not the dumb animals sometimes posited by academia and science. In life, self-experience is the one valid common denominator for reality. It is far more important than labels, which are often illusory. People might be quite uneducated when it comes to understanding what labels mean or imply and feel themselves to be inferior to someone who can adroitly manipulate them. In the long run, people who are dominated by labels and have little self-experience about what they actually mean are probably the least truly educated.

Self-experience is the only way to know true reality. It is self-experience that leads to common sense, which is always superior to label manufacturing. In fact, self-experience and enlightenment go hand in hand.

This is especially true of ESP. Extrasensory perception has one strong dominant feature that has been ignored. Like eating, sleeping, having sex, or thought imaging, it is always an *experience* and never just a label. It may be a giddy, unnerving, confusing, or sublime experience, but an experience it is. In other words, all the known forms of ESP are psychic-metabolic functions of one kind or another that deliver themselves up into consciousness as self-experience.

True extrasensory perception cannot be contacted in the representational universe using only the labels we have arbitrarily assigned to it. It can be contacted only in the experiential universe—and then only within *its own* terms and rules.

So the new stage I'd like to set for ESP is one that has self-experience as the major prerequisite for any real understanding of ESP functioning.

RW (REASONS WHY)

TWO

ESP—A Redefinition

Extrasensory perception normally means perception of those things and phenomena that reside beyond or outside the ordinary senses. Dr. J. B. Rhine made the term familiar in the United States when he published his monograph *Extrasensory Perception* in 1937. This was followed in 1940 by *Extrasensory Perception after Sixty Years*. The term caught the public imagination, and soon ESP was a household word.

In the context of Rhine's use of the term, it referred to something quite precise: scientifically controlled laboratory experimentation. It did not refer to the human self-experience of extrasensory phenomena, but only to a study of them.

A good synopsis of how this came to be is given in the *Encyclopedia of Occultism and Parapsychology*:

> Much of the transition from the Psychical Science of the 1900s to the Parapsychology of the last few decades has been largely only a semantic revolution, riddled with initialisms like ESP

and PK as well as statistical analysis of laboratory tests, giving an air of respectability to what was formerly regarded as a very dubious affair of phenomena associated with mediums and Spiritualism. In the process of making psychical phenomena safe for science, and therefore deserving of grants and sponsorships, the emphasis shifted initially to laboratory tests with card-guessing and dice-rolling, where experiments could be evaluated statistically.*

The particular nuance of ESP given by Rhine was one of scientific distinction. Rhine did not originate the term. It had been used in Europe in the 1920s, specifically by Dr. Rudolf Tischner, an ophthalmologist of Munich, who also conducted research into occult and psychical phenomena. Tischner used the term in close connection with "externalization of sensibility," which goes back to 1892, when the French researcher Dr. Paul Joire first used it to describe the phenomenon of an individual's being able to sense something outside the skin of the body without the apparent use of any of the known physical senses.

Joire had observed this phenomenon particularly with subjects who were in a trance or hypnotized. They could sense objects outside their body even at some distance, in another room with the door closed between. The presence of this phenomenon led to the idea that there was some component of the human body or human mind that could self-project outside the body and perceive or sense objects or events at a distance.

This idea seemed to be adequately confirmed. Trance states and hypnotic phenomena were deeply studied during the latter nineteenth century and the first decades of the twentieth. It was found that certain individuals were adept at externalization. With their body supine on a

*See *Encyclopedia of Occultism and Parapsychology*, Gale Research Company, Detroit, 1978, under the heading "Parapsychology," p. 692.

couch, they could project through walls, go down streets, and see what was happening in a friend's kitchen several blocks away, narrating their experiences as they did so.

Some of these feats are quite incredible, and it seems they weren't all that rare. Any serious student of ESP will eventually want to read the reports of these events as collected by Dr. Eric J. Dingwall in five volumes under the somewhat misleading title *Abnormal Hypnotic Phenomena*.*

The term "externalization of sensibility" fell into disuse with the rise of the popular term "extrasensory perception." Yet if we closely examine the two, we can discern a significant difference between them.

Extrasensory perception is a neutral scientific label that does not evoke much beyond its definition. Externalization of sensibility is a phenomenological term, an active term that evokes many different kinds of intuitive associations. How many of us have been able to sense external things or events at a distance? Sense danger around the corner? Sense that loved ones are in trouble across the continent? Externalization of sensing plunges deeper into the core of self-experience than does extrasensory perception, which is more a mental label. It is too bad that externalization of sensibility was not carried forward into contemporary parapsychology, for if it had been, the overall picture would by now be quite different. Extrasensory perception is closely connected to statistical analysis of minimal ESP events, while external *sensing* evokes intuition and self-experience. Working with these two terms shows that extrasensory perception is a head- or mind-oriented concept, whereas external sensing evokes a holistic experiential mode. If this shift in nuance is troublesome, you can always consider the facts. Telling someone to use his ESP, as it is currently defined, seldom produces any

*Eric J. Dingwall, *Abnormal Hypnotic Phenomena*, J. & A. Churchill, London, 1967. Volume IV is published by Barnes & Noble, 1968.

notable ESP. You will have much more luck if you focus on external sensing. A whole gamut of psychic self-experience will shortly become available to you, even if you have not already encountered some before.

If we consider these two terms together (as they should be), we still have only one end of a definition. We can see there is some function that "goes out" and senses things and events outside the capability of the limited physical senses. The other end of our definition has to consider what "comes in." There is a great yawning vacuum in contemporary parapsychology about this, but it is a part of psychical research that has been considered by a few pre-parapsychology researchers.

One of the truly epochal studies of the overall psychic experience was published in 1923 by Dr. Eugene Osty (at that time the director of the Institut Metapsychique International in Paris). In French, the book was titled *La Connaissance Supranormale*. It covers several saga-like instances in which Osty tested gifted mediums or medium-type individuals who were able to sense events far away from themselves, and also sense into the future. But Osty went one step further. He made an attempt to give form to what was happening when the individuals were making their efforts.

His conclusions are encapsulated in the French title. We can now witness one of those semantic flip-flops that take place when people are not sure of what they are talking about. When Osty's book was translated into English by Stanley de Brath, it came out under the title *Supernormal Faculties in Man*.* Frankly, this is a gross mistranslation of the worst kind, but it was one that fitted neatly into the science semantics of the English language, giving the English version a more "scientific" frame of reference.

Supranormale means beyond the normal, while *la*

---

*Eugene Osty, *Supernormal Faculties in Man*, Methuen & Co., London, 1923.

connaissance means knowledge, information, understanding, learning, idea, and familiarity.

A literal rendering of the title is supranormal knowledge or supranormal information. This is in keeping with the major hypothesis of Osty's book: that there exists knowledge and information in some kind of supranormal state which individuals can tap into via *their* supranormal senses In other words what "comes in" to the mind of the individual is information and knowledge, learning, familiarity, ideas, and understanding. Osty speculates only on the "how" of all this, but he does establish that humans possess some sensing mechanisms that "go out" and connect on a supranormal level with information that "comes in." When Osty's remarkable book is read with this in mind, it comes as a revelation justly deserving the plaudits that were given it.

If we put all these considerations together, we can evolve a new definition for ESP: What we call extrasensory perception is the result of an external sensing by which information and knowledge is contacted and, through subliminal processes, brought into consciousness, without the use of any of the known physical senses. The following chart illustrates all this in a general sense.

It is worth noting that modern Russian scientists have coined a term that incorporates all these facets quite well— they use the term "extrasensory perception" only rarely. Their term is "bioinformation." This has the advantage of cutting beneath all the arbitrary labels Westerners habitually use to describe phenomena such as clairvoyance, precognition, telepathy, and ESP. There is by now very little justification for separating "bioinformation" in this manner, since all parapsychology's attempts to do so have proved fruitless.

The use of bioinformation has one truly great advantage. It focuses the individual's attention on getting "information" rather than upon some hypothetical faculty that might be implied by ESP.

E S P   R E S U L T

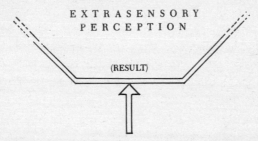

E X T R A S E N S O R Y
P E R C E P T I O N

(RESULT)

E X T E R I O R I Z A T I O N   O F   S E N S I B I L I T Y

(PSYCHIC PROCESSES)
(PRECONSCIOUS)

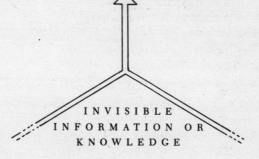

I N V I S I B L E
I N F O R M A T I O N   O R
K N O W L E D G E

The step the Russians took in coining their new word
was really quite brilliant. It is (at the present time, anyway) much easier to divide information into categories
than it is to divide up the psychic faculties that acquire the
information.

In fact, I've used the Russian approach to support my
own experience and learning since I first became aware of
their research in 1975. Using information as the key, ESP
can generally be divided into three categories. I call them
hard-wired, semisoft-wired, and soft-wired.

<u>Hard-wired ESP</u> concerns a sensing of a physical object
or event in a circumstance where the truthfulness of what
was sensed can be proved by objective fact. For example,
if after you try to perceive by psychic means something on
a table in another room, you can go see what was on the
table; if your effort proves correct, then there has been a
"hard wiring" between your ESP biosensing systems and
the object on the table.

An example of <u>semisoft-wired ESP</u> is the "receiving" of
a new idea (information, knowledge) to complete a new
project or invention, or perhaps to conceive a new invention altogether. The needed idea-information-knowledge
"arrives" in your ESP biosensing systems from an unknown place. You can then materialize the project or
invention in fact. The result is objective and demonstrable.

Soft-wired ESP involves those areas that cannot be demonstrated in any objective form. They are philosophical or
metaphysical in nature—talking with the Masters, tapping
the akashic* records, seeing new visions on how the universe is put together (without subsequent proof that it is

---

*The akashic records is a corruption of the Sanskrit word Ākāśa which, in
ancient Hindu mysticism, referred to the primeval element that existed
before the physical creation out of chaos of the cosmos. It is homogeneous or
undifferentiated, but is thought to carry an imprint of everything that has
existed or happened since Creation. Some psychics feel they can consult
these imprints in certain conditions of consciousness, hence the idea of
"records." The Hebrew Old Testament refers to Ākāśa as the "kosmic
Waters." Contemporary quantum physics is struggling with a concept that is
analogous to Ākāśa.

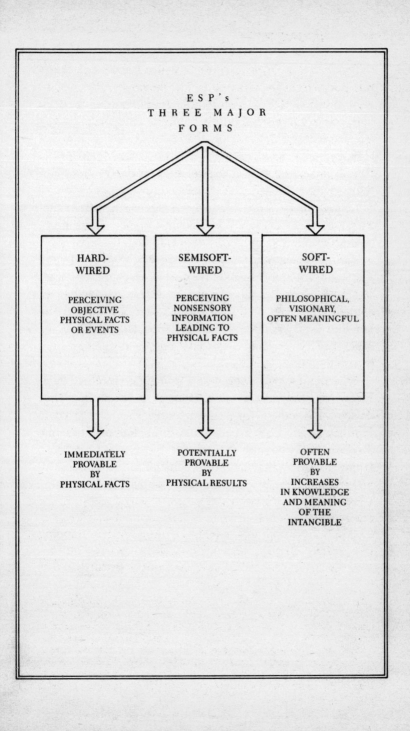

so), prophecies or precognitions that do not fulfill themselves, experiencing other entities or beings on other planes. Should any soft ESP factor fulfill itself in some form, it would be, of course, semisoft.

Hard-wired ESP is immediately provable in physical terms.

Semisoft-wired ESP is eventually provable.

Soft-wired ESP—?

Each of these three categories depends upon the validity of the information they contain, as the chart given above shows.

Natural ESP concerns itself specifically with hard-wired ESP biosensing because it is capable of repetitive trials followed by immediate feedback. These will help you contact your own ESP core piecemeal and let you build familiarity and confidence in it. Once this is done, the other two types stand a good chance of developing on a firmer footing.

When I first volunteered as a psychic research subject, I did not understand these nuances or even that they existed. I began in the worst possible state and tried to fulfill my own ESP expectations through the labels that are commonly in use. Yet almost by chance, I made a major discovery that served to connect me to some hard-wired *connaissance supranormale*, which I'll describe in Chapter 4.

△ THREE △

The Extrasensory
Mind Mound

Our setting for a new approach to ESP will look barren if it has a single backdrop made only of the potential for people to experience ESP.

There is nothing on this backdrop yet, but so far we can understand why the stage should be emptied of scenery and props left over from past productions that attempted to enact ESP. Those productions closed down after limited runs.

To begin to construct the scenery necessary, let's start with an assumption that *may* be true: that extrasensory perception and the mind are probably inseparable. Without a mind (or brain) upon which to register its astonishing and transrational activities, who could ever say whether or not ESP existed in the first place? We can refine this a little, and say that extrasensory perception registers its information in those awarenesses that are prepared to receive it, or are not blocked from doing so.

Thus, the territories of our minds should make up the basic scenery of our new ESP. We have to describe this, but in terms that can be self-experienced and not in labels that prohibit experience. Psychology has evolved a lot of labels for various aspects of the mind, only some of which are useful for our purposes.

If we were to use these labels for our ESP stage, it would look strange indeed, and quite unaesthetic. Over here would be a label for ego, and over there would be a label for unconscious, and somewhere else would be the label for superconscious, and perhaps additional labels for consciousnesses 1, 2, and 3. We might slip in labels for soul, dreams, spontaneous experience, reverie, altered states 1 through 20.

We could *read* these labels, but nothing in them would help us experience what they mean. What we need in order to evoke the self-experience of our minds are constructs that we can intuitively identify with, that have a ring of truth in them. We cannot simply say, "Self-experience your mind." It doesn't work that way, even though we are experiencing it every moment of our lives. We need to cause parts of the mind to resonate with objective words, to reveal themselves as real, and for that realness to be intimately familiar to us all.

About the only way to do this is through the use of analogies. There are many we could use, but I ran across one that seems particularly suitable. It has three advantages: It does not utilize labels, it is not disprovable by psychology, and it evokes experiential response.

It was written in 1904 by the psychologist Denton J. Snider, in a book with the long title, *Feeling Psychologically Treated and Prolegomena to Psychology*. Snider's book is a wonderful excursion into the phenomenology of the mind as it more or less existed *before* Freudianism (which gave us so many labels) came into domination and before the rise of specialized mechanistic psychologies (which gave us many more). Snider wrote:

> Taken in its literal simplicity, Psychology signifies the science of the Soul, or of the Mind.

Even such a definition gives to it a broad sweep which has been narrowed in various ways by different writers, who have in them the prevalent bent toward specialization. At the present time, the most common view of Psychology holds it to be the science of the phenomena of the mind, such as perception, sensation, memory, which this science finds and picks up (so to speak), and then proceeds to describe and to put into some kind of order. As there are phenomena of Nature with which physical science deals, so there are phenomena of Mind with which psychological science deals. As there are classes of flowers, so there are classes of mental activities; as there are strata of the earth in geology, so there are strata of the mind. Next we may note the difference between the two kinds of phenomena. The geologist perceives the stratum and arranges it according to his scheme; but if he perceives himself perceiving the stratum, he no longer geologizes but psychologizes. The moment his mind passes from regarding the outer object to regarding its own activity he changes to a new field which has its distinct science. A wholly different set of phenomena rises to view.

Snider's "distinct science" is, of course, built upon distinct experience. I think we can all agree, if we try to observe the workings of our own minds, that in them we can experience classes or even species of mental activities. Beyond the classes of awake mental activities, we can also experience deeper strata or levels in our minds. We already know which of these strata are frilly and which are profound. We are aware of sinking through strata when we meditate or fall asleep, and rising through levels when we approach wakefulness.

We can add to Snider's two qualities another called boundaries, and say that like things in nature that have different boundaries, the mind can experience different boundaries. When we drink too much, have a peak experience, take a psychoactive drug, or experience a wonderful symphony or rock group, we can experience our mind's boundaries changing.

We don't necessarily need labels for these mentally experienced phenomena. They go on all the time inside our minds with or without names for them.

It is these different classes of mental activities, the different mental strata, and the different changing mental boundaries that will make up the scenery on our new stage. Extrasensory perceptions work and function among all these, and it is among these that we can experience firsthand the elements of extrasensory perception and its many different qualities. Somewhere in each of us is a particular classification of all these that I would like to call the "extrasensory mind mound." This term is dangerously close to being yet another label, but not exactly so. It is an allegorical label which tells an experiential story, rather than an intellectual label which is empty of experience.

The extrasensory mind mound is like one of those huge mounds found in the deserts of Turkey, the plains of the American Midwest, or the jungles of Mexico. Outwardly, the mound has trees and shrubs on it, and it rises a hundred or so feet into the air, resembling a hill. Sometimes these mounds served as dumping grounds, and small relics are found—a pottery cup, an arrowhead, a small carved idol.

When archaeologists begin digging into the hill, it is not a hill at all, but the remains of a fortress city, a majestic burial ground, or a large temple. Slicing into the mound, the archaeologist finds the foundations, the rooms, the arts, the ancient inscriptions. From these clues, the archaeologist can recreate the life-styles of the former inhabitants, and begin to intuit their motives and goals which had for centuries remained invisible, unknown, and intangible.

With regard to extrasensory perception, though we do not think of a shrub-covered mound in a desert or plain, we have to envision a mound in the mind, because ESP is a mental craft or art. This mind mound lurks in the planes or levels of the mind. Its shrubbery is that of ideas about the nature of ESP that have collected upon its surface. Its artifacts are spontaneous ESP experiences or lab results which really cannot be explained any more than the pottery shards and small idols—not, at least, until the mound itself is penetrated.

In spite of the artifacts on the surface of this mind mound, no one has dug a trench into it, sliced into its core. And so its internal secrets remain covered by its outside accumulations.

ESP Processes Are Invisible

The psychic processes in the mind mound are normally invisible to our direct mental perception. They probably function in the preconscious or unconscious parts of our mind. When we do undergo an extrasensory experience, what we become aware of are the *results* of those invisible processes poking up into our awake consciousness.

The normal way of dealing with invisibles is to compare them to something that *is* visible or tangible, or at least thinkable. That brings the invisible into a state our conscious, thinking awareness can deal with intellectually. But it should be borne in mind that these are only temporary references made up for the convenience of conscious awareness. They still cloak the invisibles beneath them.

The term "extrasensory perception" is a label that covers an invisible, which in turn covers several other invisibles, such as clairvoyance, telepathy, precognition, and remote viewing. An individual "sees" an activity taking

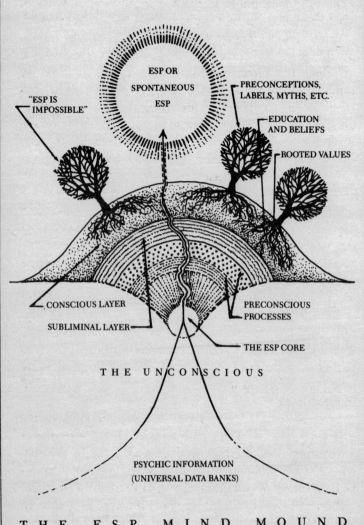

CONSCIOUSNESS—AND AWARENESS

ESP OR
SPONTANEOUS
ESP

"ESP IS
IMPOSSIBLE"

PRECONCEPTIONS,
LABELS, MYTHS, ETC.

EDUCATION
AND BELIEFS

ROOTED VALUES

CONSCIOUS LAYER

PRECONSCIOUS
PROCESSES

SUBLIMINAL LAYER

THE ESP CORE

THE UNCONSCIOUS

PSYCHIC INFORMATION
(UNIVERSAL DATA BANKS)

THE ESP MIND MOUND

place a thousand miles away, and when this is confirmed, people say, "Ah, that was clairvoyance." This is good only so far as it goes, but it doesn't tell us anything at all about what happened during the process labeled "clairvoyance."

From the beginning of organized inquiry into human psychic phenomena, extrasensory perception was expected to mimic the physical senses; that is, through ESP we would "see" as our eyes see, "hear" as our ears hear, and "feel" as our tactile senses feel. There was some justification for this expectation because in examples of high-stage ESP, this was indeed the case. The percipient (the one having the ESP experience) sometimes had ESP impressions so clear and precise that it seemed he *was* seeing with his eyes.

When this *is* the case, it is easy enough to understand the mistake in thinking that ESP processes *always* work that way. In reality all we have is the *result* of the invisible processes spontaneously functioning in their high-stage condition. This high-stage functioning serves to confirm our expectations and reinforces our thinking that the result is ESP itself. All this leads us *away* from any contact with the invisible processes that *produced* this kind of result. As we shall see, ESP is actually several different kinds of processes, a series of "mind manifestations" that invisibly take place when an individual is endeavoring to use ESP in some form.

While we will delve into specific aspects of the invisible ESP processes, we don't want to lose track of the greater implications. Specifically, we don't want to make the mistake that has so often been made—we don't want to detach the ESP *result* from the greater invisible psychic system and put it by itself under the magnifying glass to the detriment of losing touch with the greater psychic realities that produced the result in the first place.

△ **FOUR** △

The ESP Experience
and the ESP Impact

S elf-experience and impact are two elements necessary to give reality to any phenomenon. Without these two elements, we can have only a shallow touch with the phenomena of life. They ground us in reality. In their absence, we have only a conception of what something is like, a conception that can be over-intellectualized and glued together with labels, all of which is likely to leave us feeling a little foolish once we come up against the real thing.

I think it should be admitted that no one can truly value extrasensory perception (or the paranormal in general) until he has experienced some phase of it. A few experiences might not lead to complete knowledge and understanding; but basic values will have shifted.

Between 1971 and the present time, I've taken part in well over a half million different kinds of ESP experiments and test trials. I've also been able to make a good survey of all the intellectual surmises that have come to surround ESP and its problems. None of these experiments and

ESP tests has been more poignant than those that began my career as a psychic test subject.

These first experiments are representative of the self-experience and impacts that anyone will experience to some degree if they use this book as a guide, and seek to touch upon their own ESP core. It was as a result of these experiments that I discovered the special elements that are the topic of this book.

In the summer of 1971, I was invited, through friends, to become a test subject at the venerable American Society for Psychical Research (ASPR) in New York. This society was first founded in 1885, and has had a variable career since then. It was established as the American counterpart to the British Psychical Research Society (SPR) founded a few years earlier in 1882. A French counterpart was formed in Paris in 1918 as the Institut Metapsychique International. These three societies are mentioned here because their archives contain much that will be discussed later on. Their common goal was to research the many different kinds of psychic phenomena, although since their founding, the direction of the research has taken different path, depending on who was at the helm.

Between 1971 and 1972, I went to the ASPR three times a week to be a "subject" in ongoing experiments. Research at that time was directed by Dr. Karlis Osis, a veteran parapsychologist born in Riga, Latvia. His assistant was Janet Mitchell, who has since earned her doctorate in parapsychology. Osis and Mitchell were involved in exploring the out-of-body experience, and they were busy recruiting guinea pigs for their tests.

At the beginning of these experiments, I believed in the existence of ESP, but did *not* believe that I possessed any particular talent for it. I was interested, however, or I would not have bothered to volunteer for the tests. It is important to emphasize this because there will be many readers in the same situation: believing in the existence of ESP, but also believing that they themselves don't possess such talents. What was to follow for me amounted to revelation, and began a psychic career that has endured for over sixteen years.

All the testing at the ASPR consisted of the standard form of concealing some object out of sight of the subject, who was then required to perceive what the object was. These objects were placed on tables in other rooms, concealed in machines, suspended in boxes from the ceiling. Sometimes they involved "target areas" at locations a distance from the ASPR, especially in rooms in the Museum of Natural History some ten city blocks away. The latter type experiment was the first long-distance one in modern times to be called "remote viewing," although, unknown to me, and generally forgotten by researchers at the time, the first "remote viewing" had already taken place some fifty-five years earlier.

The principal method Dr. Osis was using to test for out-of-body perception consisted of placing some targets flat on a tray box which was then suspended two feet beneath the high-ceilinged experimental room. An eight-stepped ladder was used to place and retrieve the targets. The subject's brain waves were being monitored by brain wave–recording equipment, and he or she was literally tied to a chair by wires. The subject could barely move without disturbing the recording machine. The goal was to "float up out of the body" and try to identify the targets lying on the tray some eight feet above the head.

The winter of 1971 was especially disagreeable, filled with days of early cold, snow, and sleet. On each day of a scheduled experiment, I'd make the long subway trip from my home to the ASPR rooms, usually arriving with a running nose. I'd sit for a half hour or more while the leads to the polygraph were pasted on various parts of my scalp, wrists, and ankles. Another lead was pasted on my finger (to measure blood pressure), while another was placed on my chest (to count heartbeats).

When all this was ready, I was led into the room where the targets were suspended from the ceiling on the tray. I

sat in a chair, and all the leads were plugged into the wall
fixture directly behind my chair. I had hardly any freedom
of movement, since any large movement created "artifacts" on the machines in the other room.

When everything was in working order, the lights were
dimmed, and I was asked to try to go out of body, float up
to the tray, and peer down at it from the ceiling. If my
nose continued to run, I was out of luck. There was no
way of reaching into my pocket for a tissue without dis-
rupting the entire EEG system.

If I merely imagined I was up at the ceiling, there was
little chance of "seeing" what was on the tray. Yet there
were all sorts of impressions whirling through my mind—
the action in the street outside the building, what was
going on in other rooms nearby, and a few fleeting images
of what I took to be views of the tray's contents. I'd try to
dictate the impressions into the intercom and tape recorder.

What was actually happening was a jumble of forms,
vague, swiftly changing, as if in my mental perceptual
apparatus there was a kaleidoscope of some kind, constantly evolving and reshaping bits and pieces of images.
Every once in a while, one of these would solidify for a
moment before vanishing. I'd become aware of colors and
different shapes existing in some kind of relationship to
each other. When I tried to verbalize these impressions,
as was the design of the experiment, a typical response
would go something like this: "Uh, I see a shape. It has
corners, but I can't tell if it is square or oblong. I'm seeing
it as a house, but I know a house can't be up there in the
box, so maybe it is a toy house. But then it's not very
thick, so maybe it's . . . [I'd draw a blank on words] . . .
next to it is something small that looks like a cross or a
safety pin, uh, I'm now seeing a diaper, but that's an obvious
association to the safety pin, uh, the square-like thing is
red-or pink and seems to be about one-half inch thick."

When the experiment was over, I was unhooked from
the electrodes and we viewed the target. It turned out to
be a small red address book (not a toy house), and next to

it was a small golden cross strung on a safety pin. But there were other things on the tray box that I hadn't perceived at all—such as a free-form cutout of paper, and a series of numbers. So part of the experiment was a success, while another part of it drew a blank.

I was disabused of any idea that my ESP was going to operate like a TV screen in my own mind, or that my out-of-body perception was going to be crystal clear. It is at this point that most people would want to give up and get back into the real world.

But Karlis Osis and Janet Mitchell were quite pleased with the results, calling them successful, when to me they were only partial results. I was encouraged to continue the experiments.

I began to take a more attentive look at what was going on in my head vis-à-vis trying to perceive the targets. One of the things that became apparent was that when I would try to identify one of the images by the word for it, attempting to dictate my responses into the tape recorder, many different words came up. And these in turn seemed to stimulate a good deal of imagery on their own.

For example, I'd get an impression of a roundish red thing. Or was it an ovalish red thing? Perhaps it's a heart-shaped cutout, no, maybe just a circle? And then there would be heart shapes and circles of all kinds whirling into my mind, even images of the St. Valentine's Day hearts I remember cutting out in the second grade in school. And circles galore. Soon I couldn't discriminate at all between the word-stimulated images and those that might truly represent the contents of the tray.

The Problem of Word Representations

I discussed this problem with the researchers, who were sympathetic to it. But narrating one's impressions into a tape recorder was the accepted way, and this required words. Even so, the targets on the tray were not composed of "words," but of shapes and forms which needed to be recognized *before* a word could be assigned correctly to them. Granted, if the out-of-body perception had the acuity of the physical eyes, then there should be no problem. But what I was perceiving were bits of shapes, forms, and colors which in themselves were not clear. Any effort to label these with a word turned them, in my mind, into many images that fit that particular word. In my mind, I would see things that obviously were not on the tray.

I began to realize that the mere action of trying to *verbalize* what I was "seeing" was an impediment because it caused the mind to manufacture far more images than were needed. These extra images flooded the perceptual ESP field with useless and inappropriate information.

My first results were, therefore, not very good. My taped verbal responses contained only a few target-related materials. I was very disappointed.

My First Picture Drawings

In between experiments, I kept thinking, "There has to be another way of doing this. . . ."

The actual idea came while riding the subway one day. In the early 1970s, the world was beginning to have to consider how to make signs that did not use words, especially in airports and train stations where people of many different languages traveled. Originating in Europe, a way had been found to make a sign that did not need its meaning translated into a half-dozen languages. A No Smoking sign was now not made up of words, but was a picture of a cigarette with an X over it. The way to the telephones was not a verbal sign, but a picture of a telephone with an arrow pointing in the appropriate direction. On the subway, the seats reserved for the handicapped had a crutch or a wheelchair painted on them. On the subway platforms, there were signs for stairs, not made up of the word "stairs," but a picture of stairs with an arrow.

At the time, these signs were novelties. But I noticed how much information was really contained in them, without the use of words.

I didn't make the connection right away, but one night it came in a dream. I dreamt of the experimental room at the ASPR filled with signs such as these.

Ah ha! I said on wakening. Is this a way to get rid of the problem of words during the experiment?

When I arrived at the ASPR that day for the experiment, I made a suggestion to Osis and Mitchell. It seemed a simple suggestion, even an inane one. Why not try to sketch what I was seeing? Instead of trying to verbalize what I was "seeing," why not just portray the shapes and figures as they were appearing to me, thereby relieving the mind of trying to transliterate them into verbal form.

When it was discovered that with a pad on my knee my small finger movements did not disrupt the brain wave charts, Osis and Mitchell accepted my suggestion.

To my utter surprise and everyone else's, this seemingly insignificant shifting from word manufacturing to picture drawing soon expanded my ESP experience from a sense of irritating futility into one of excitement and hope. The new picture-drawing method produced results of quite some excellence, and we were, so to speak, "cooking with gas."

ESP Impact

In November and December of 1971, I began using picture drawings to record my psychic impressions of the targets concealed in the tray box suspended from the ceiling. There was an immediate shift in the quality of the psychic responses, of which I want to show you two examples.

On November 24, 1971, I arrived at the ASPR with a light case of the flu, and the experiment transcript indicates that I did the actual experiment with a runny nose, and that my ears were ringing. When I felt I had exteriorized my senses from the body and "floated up" to the ceiling, I perceived two objects lying in the tray box. I made a quick picture drawing of them, which took about thirty seconds.

Below is a sketch of the actual targets lying in the tray box.

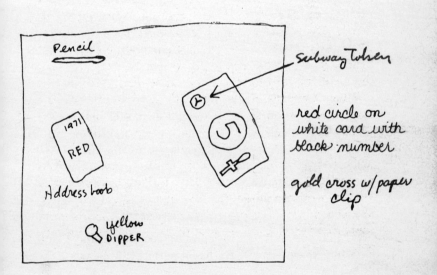

You will see that the targets consisted of eight separate elements: a pencil, a yellow plastic dipper, a red 1971 address book, a white card upon which were placed a subway token, a cross on a safety pin (again), and a red circle with a black number five on it.

My picture drawing response is shown below.

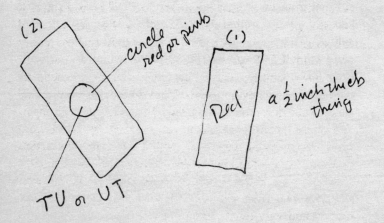

circle
red or pink

(2)

(1)

Red

a $\frac{1}{2}$ inch thick
thing

TU or UT

You will note that I did not "see" several of the items:
the pencil, the yellow plastic dipper, the token, or the
cross. I perceived the red square shape of the 1971 date
book and gave its correct thickness. Next to it, I drew the
oblong shape of the white card and correctly identified the
red circle with a figure on it. This was given as an tu or a
UT. We were all astonished with this because *if* I had
added just one more very small line connecting the U to
the T forms, we would have had a perfect number 5.

UT = UT or 5

As a result of this particular experiment, I began to feel sure that there indeed existed a hidden extrasensory perceptual system that functioned with rules and a logic of its own. My sense of awe increased, and I began to find it necessary to deal with the implications. For one thing, if this were true, it actually meant that we *do* possess a very basic kind of ESP system that lies within us in an undeveloped form simply, and for no other reason, because its elements have never been acknowledged in their actual state. They have been seen only in a spontaneous form, and those forms have been represented by labels and words that do not serve very well to describe the actual structure of this hidden extrasensory perceptual system. I reasoned that if this system *can be allowed* to function along its own rules and logic, it must be capable of very refined and very exact perception.

The clincher came during the experiment of December 30, 1971. As a result of it, my life was never to be the same.

I remember the day well. There were light snow showers, but it was not cold. I felt good and was eager. Yet when I had produced my picture drawing, I felt a sense of disappointment. It looked much like the others, and I wondered if they had perhaps used the same number 5 target again. I'd come to expect several objects in the tray, but in this case I perceived only one. Here is my picture drawing:

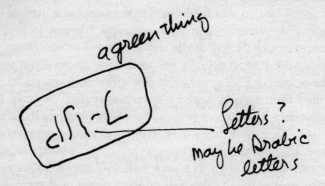

It was a few moments before the targets could be lifted down, and then we peered into the tray box. There were three items and a row of numbers that I had not perceived at all, and there was certainly nothing with Arabic letters on it.

It was Dr. Osis who first made the connection. "Ingo," he said in his charming Latvian accent, "if you turn your drawing upside down and look at it, you have drawn a perfect rendering of the 7-UP can."

And so it was. What I had seen as Arabic letters was actually 7-UP upside down.

After this day's work was done and we all had congratulated ourselves on a fine result, I recall that I got to the subway entrance. It was snowing lightly, and frankly, I was thrilled. Going down the stairs, the full impact hit me.

There actually existed a "psychic mind"!

Somewhere in my mental makeup was a psychic element—which I later termed the "ESP core"—that was capable of perceiving a hidden target and conveying a good deal of information, *without* having to employ intellectual word manufacturing. That is to say, without the intervention of consciousness, which, in any case, was so stupid as not to be able to immediately recognize 7-UP because the psychic mind had caused it to be drawn upside down.

Many things went through my head during that long pause on the subway stairs, along with the waves of goosebumps that were cascading along my spine. What were the implications of all this? What did it mean that unbeknownst to my conscious mind there existed a hidden level within me that was capable of extrasensory contact with an equally hidden target?

This hidden level was alien to what I had *learned* about ESP from reading books. It simply didn't fit with what I had expected. Yet the results were there, and continued to develop during the following experiments. The ESP mind was not part of the conscious mind, and hence had never been truly touched through conscious intellectualizing and labels. In fact, only the shift from conscious word manufacturing to semiconscious or spontaneous picture drawing had made it visible, and that shift was the result of a fluke. My God, I thought, if this can be developed, what are the implications?

As my moments of ESP impact came to a close, I once again became aware of the people passing, the pre–New Year's rush. I was simply astonished.

During the days that followed, I wondered if I was the first person to use picture drawings. I earnestly hoped that others *had* used them, because I would then be able to compare my work to theirs—and hopefully learn something more about this hidden ESP level.

Once you know what you are looking for, research is not all that difficult. During 1972, I found that there had indeed been picture drawings before mine, and that some of the most notable had been achieved *at the very beginning* of organized psychical research in the nineteenth century. And yet no particular importance had ever been attached to them; they existed in the journals and books as just curiosa.

At the close of 1971, one thing had become clear to me. The psychic system at the core of the extrasensory mind mound needed to be freed of all the other mind manifestations that impeded a clear perceiving of the basic primary extrasensory perceptions. And the way to do this was to set aside all that I thought ESP was, eject the many labels under which my conscious expectations worked, and study the elements contained in the picture drawings themselves.

In this way, my ESP core eventually opened itself to me and my conscious mind had new experience-oriented information with which it eventually established new values and appreciation for raw extrasensory perception.

△ FIVE △

The Extrasensory You

In the course of the last fifteen years, I've crawled through *all* the published journals of psychical research and parapsychology published in English and French. I've also read several hundred books, looking for descriptions of what was going on in the head of a person experiencing ESP, especially the hard-wired type. My experiences at the ASPR in 1971 stimulated many questions, and one of these was whether or not any previous psychic subjects had experienced the same kind of phenomena I had. At first I expected to find reports detailing how a subject felt while undergoing the psychic experience. But it quickly became apparent that if such reports did exist, they were few and far between.

I could find no catalogue or index heading that made this search easy. So in exasperation, I finally sat down and started with the first journals and proceedings published by the British Psychical Research Society in 1882 and methodically worked my way through them and the publications of the other research groups founded after that date.

41

Missing in this grand archive is a category of reports detailing what is happening to a subject in his or her own head during the time the ESP experience is taking place. I strongly believe that the head experience of a subject—especially a successful subject—is of primary importance for anyone truly wanting to be in touch with the fundamental workings of the external sensing.

This gaping hole is not noticed until it is pointed out, and then it plunges like a bottomless crevasse in the standard research methods that have been traditionally utilized in parapsychology and its predecessor, psychical research.

Throughout the years, I've asked several leading parapsychologists about this omission. Generally they do not consider it an omission, but a matter of form. The form goes something like this: The subject is usually not a trained scientist himself and so cannot be a credible witness to *his own* inner processes. Only trained researchers detached from the object they are studying can be credible witnesses, even if they have to try to view ESP phenomena secondhand through their detached observations.

Another reason, lurking behind the scenes, is that when some subjects try to volunteer information about their ESP experience, from their point of view, what they say often differs radically from what the researchers think is going on. When this happens, it amounts to label blasting and the entire hypothesis upon which parapsychology is mounted starts quivering accordingly.

Some parapsychologists will interpret these comments in an antagonistic way, insisting that they *have* been interested in the internal workings of their subjects. To some degree this is true. I, myself, have been asked what I experience during a given experiment. Only four parapsychologists have been truly interested, however, while many of the others seemed to listen to my reports only out of politeness. For the most part, there has been no interest at all. I've been very vocal, during my career, about the importance of the subject's self-experiences. On one occasion, as I was getting ready to travel to act as a subject for J. B. Rhine, I got a telephone report from a friend. During the preexperiment briefing with his staff, Rhine had pointed out that if they *had* to listen to my ideas in order to get me to come and act as a subject, everyone was to pretend interest, but that my ideas were not to be listened to otherwise.

The fact remains that in official experimental reports, there is no category entitled "What the subject says he experiences during the ESP experience." This category should belong in any report of an ESP experiment in which a human has been used as a test subject.

Reporting only on what the experimentor can observe or deduce (the experimentor's space) is really only half the experiment. What is going on in the subject's head (the subject's space) constitutes the other half. Yet after a hundred years, the subject is still being poked and prodded with instruments and research ideas *only*. This is like finding an obviously animate blob in one's backyard, poking it with a stick, and then looking first to see what happened to the stick. But the blob might possibly be an extraterrestrial intelligence dropping in. The first line of human response is not to get into communication: "Say, there, can you speak and tell us something?" No, the blob can expect only to get prodded with another stick, somewhat along the lines of the standard human hypothesis that when you find something strange, shoot first and dissect later.

By way of giving an example of the one-sidedness of experimental reports, Dr. Osis published a short informal report of eight consecutive experiments I had taken part in during 1971 and 1972, experiments exactly along the lines of those described in the preceding chapter. Osis and Mitchell were prevented from publishing an official report in their society's journal because the publishing committee had never encountered such a successful run of experiments and felt that if they published the results officially, the society would suffer undue attacks from skeptics.

In the general outrage that followed the handing down of this decision, Osis resorted to publishing his report in the *ASPR Newsletter*, No. 14, Summer 1972.

Osis gives the results from a blind judging of the eight sets of experimental materials (rejudged five times thereafter) as being statistically relevant (as "the likelihood of getting 8 out of 8 by chance is 1 in approximately 40,000"). He then talks about perception achieved during the experiments, whether or not OOB (out-of-body) vision follows the laws of optics. He then goes into physiology: "What is happening to Ingo Swann's body at the time when he feels his spiritual self to be somewhere else?" and he describes what my brainwaves were seen to be doing during the experiment.

Nowhere in this brief report does he mention the fact that it was the shift from verbalizing to picture drawing that was the key ingredient for achieving the eight significant results. And nowhere in this report is there any mention of what was going on in the subject's space while these remarkable results were being achieved. In short, save for its brevity and its appearance in the *Newsletter*, it is a standard report.

Separating the researcher's observational space from the subject's active psychic space serves only to bring about a trenchant artificiality into the entire proceedings. Common sense indicates that if the subject's psychic space holds the key to any deeper understanding of the extrasensory processes, then there ought to be a very close and intimate sharing of that space between subject and researcher.

I've come to term the person's psychic space as "the extrasensory you" or "the extrasensory me," if you like. Only by becoming aware of *the extrasensory you* can you start to locate the *processes* that are taking place in your ESP core, which is deeply buried in the ESP mind mound. If you want to begin taking control of your externalizing abilities, some focus has to be applied to how the internal mechanisms are working, in addition to what is trying to be sensed.

The rest of this book will make all this a little easier for you, if you make the effort to try your own simple ESP experiments. But the concept of *the extrasensory you* is of primary importance, and to acknowledge its existence is a good portion of our reorientation about ESP abilities in general.

△ **SIX** △

The Psychic Nucleus, the Deeper Self, and the ESP Core

*The secret of the clairvoyant's power may consist in the fact that he or she is able to effect a momentary form of fusion or collaboration between the conscious mind and the secret self.**

The Second Reality

The greatest drawback to any progress in comprehending extrasensory perception, at the individual level and in parapsychology, is trying to make ESP fit into the reality we think is the only reality. We are used to viewing the physical realities with our consciousness. What we can perceive with our physical senses and what we can think about with only our conscious minds has come to constitute the one and only reality.

*Leo Talamonti, *Forbidden Universe*, Stein and Day, New York, 1975, p. 44.

The other parts of our minds—the unconscious or the supraconscious, for example—predominantly have been thought *not* to have any reality of their own, but to exist in some sort of a subjective arrangement that depends upon our consciously perceived reality. This label-like concept needs to be disposed of in short order, and we can do so by making three statements about it.

First, it is a concept that is peculiar only to Westernized science and its ideas of enlightenment. Second, there is hardly any other culture that has entertained this polarized concept, much less clung so tenaciously to it. Third, two branches of Western science—quantum physics and psychology—have reached a point where evidence clearly indicates the existence of another reality.

The late 1970s and the 1980s have seen several culture-shaking books come into print that posit the existence of this second reality. These books, and many scientific papers, have not been authored by fringe kooks detached from serious science, but by highly achieved scientists exceedingly expert in their different fields.

Some fifty years ago it began to be apparent, to physicists studying the quantum fabric of the universe, that our known physical universe has, beneath it, another universe. This second universe is peculiar: It is, first of all, *nonmaterial;* yet, all things material seem to be derived from it, and this second universe has qualities that are quite contrary to our standard notions of time and space. Einstein was among the first to speculate on its potentials, but in the 1920s, the physicist Werner von Heisenberg developed his "uncertainty principle" (or indeterminancy principle) that showed that the laws of physics should be turned into statements about relative probabilities instead of absolute certainties. In 1926, Heisenberg developed a form of quantum theory known as matrix mechanics, which was quickly shown to be fully equivalent to the "wave mechanics" of another noted physicist, Erwin Schrödinger. This early work opened the door upon the other invisible and nonmaterial universe; matrix mechanics and wave mechanics have fertilized and inspired deeper inquiries into the fabric of this largely unmapped cosmic whole. During the last ten years, many books have appeared that give the layperson a chance of grasping some of the fundamentals involved. Some of these works are: David Bohm's *Wholeness and the Implicate Order;* J. L. Mackie's *The Cement of the Universe;* Paul Davies's ironically titled book *The Accidental Universe,* which marvels at the astonishing precision of the other universe; N. Katherine Hayles's *The Cosmic Web,* which is a review of scientific field models relevant to this new universe. Fritjof Capra's *The Tao of Physics: An Exploration of the Parallels between Modern Physics and Eastern Mysticism* is cast against this new universe, as is Rupert Sheldrake's bestselling book *A New Science of Life.*

All these books seek to show that the material universe, as we know it in all its divisions, is itself interlocked in some kind of fundamental, invisible harmony that holds it together with precision. This harmony is variously called implicate order, universal glue or cement, wave or field models, a cosmic web, and so forth. But they all refer to the invisible gigantic sub- or second universe that unites all things, great or small, into a "cosmic" whole.

It is worth noting that parapsychologists (especially in the United States) and their financial benefactors have been exceedingly slow in incorporating this new wave of understanding into their workings. When significant funding is made available, the largest portion of it is poured into efforts to continue the process of trying to find ESP within the old reality framework. The physical brain continues to be probed, and electromagnetism continues to be thought of as the carrier of ESP "signals," while all along, new wave research in physics has virtually established the fact that there is a second reality that operates *totally independently* of any brain-electromagnetic arrangement. In fact, the old reality pales in importance if the basic elements of the new second reality are grasped.

At first, it might seem that the elements of this second reality will be difficult to grasp. This is not the case at all. The second reality is actually quite accessible intuitively. The only difficulty has been trying to make it fit into the old framework.

As far as extrasensory perception is concerned, one of the first cracks to appear in the standard approaches to ESP and testing for it came in the 1920s as a result of the exhaustive work on telepathy done by the Russian researcher L. L. Vasiliev, a professor of physiology at the University of Leningrad.

Vasiliev's seminal book was first published in 1962 by the Leningrad State University, with an English version reaching the West in 1976.*

Vasiliev's first hypothesis was to discover how telepathy corresponded to electromagnetism, thought at that time to be the carrier of telepathic signals or information from the brain-mind of a "sender" to the brain-mind† of a "receiver." The sender was isolated in chambers of different kinds, as was the receiver, and the distance between them was sometimes as great as twelve hundred miles. As Vasiliev put it, the purpose of the telepathy study was to determine, as far as possible, its physical basis. What were the wavelengths of the electromagnetic radiation that pro-

---

*L. L. Vasiliev, *Experiments in Distant Influence*, E. P. Dutton & Co., New York, 1976.

†The current trend in brain-mind research has begun to question the idea that the mind is the same as the brain. Vasiliev, along with Penfield in the U.S., was among the first to postulate that the mind might not exist in the brain and parts of the mind might well be external to the physical body. But at least, brain and mind are no longer synonymous, and have broken apart. In terms of telepathy though, it is now thought that brains themselves are not telepathic, but that they do act as a central processing center of information picked up by the mind which is telepathic, so that the subject (receiver) can render his response into language or drawing. In this new context, we are obliged to use the new term "the brain-mind system." And, in fact, such is the title of Marilyn Ferguson's very widely read *Brain-Mind Bulletin*.

duced "mental radio," the transmission of information from one brain to another?

Vasiliev was eventually able to demonstrate that no electromagnetic shielding could prevent telepathy from taking place. "The analogy between the telepathic sender and a radio transmitter of electromagnetic waves, and the percipient as a receiver is inaccurate. . . ." Vasiliev also noted instances where "reception" sometimes took place before "transmission." There was no known apparatus or concept that could account for a telepathic receiver receiving communications before they were sent.

He then speculated that the sender would be something more like a tuning fork by which the receiver's thoughts are tuned, which is not the result of psychical processes per se, but must be attributed rather to their underlying energetic processes. He concluded that attempting to make telepathy fit into prevailing electromagnetic ideas only made it more problematical.[*]

Between the 1930s and the 1970s, while American parapsychologists were still testing for ESP with cards and dice, and trying to locate a psychophysical link in the brain to explain ESP, the Russians abandoned much of standard parapsychology and brought into existence an entirely new field called "psychoenergetics," a field that has been hot on the traces of the energetic processes that underlie the psychical processes themselves.

Just how far the Russians had run with their new ball, psychoenergetics, did not become clear in the West until a new book was translated into English in 1982. It was authored by the now famous Russian geomagnetobiologists A. P. Dubrov and V. N. Pushkin.[†]

As given in their book, the overview of ESP and psi now held by the Russians is quite dissimilar from the prevailing old ideas still clung to by much of the West.

*Ibid., p. 178.
†A. P. Dubrov and V. N. Pushkin, *Parapsychology and Contemporary Science*, Consultants Bureau, New York and London, 1982.

According to our understanding of the universe, which scientists have constructed over centuries and which therefore, seems perfectly natural to us, individual objects exist separately from each other. They connect with other objects only when they enter into a mechanical or field interaction. Similarly, we believe that peoples' and animals' brains are discrete and separate from each other. We believe all animals, including man, may interact only through sensory communication: sounds, written messages, special signals, etc.

In recent years, sub-atomic physics have been undermining this concept of nature. . . . According to this new development in physics, elementary particles have the characteristics of both corpuscular bodies and waves. That is, a particle with wave properties is not located in a particular, strictly determined place; as a wave, it can be all over the entire universe or at different points at the same time.

Obviously, this non-localized physics destroys our customary concept that the universe is made up of discrete objects which occupy specific locations in space and interact only under certain conditions.*

Expanding their hypothesis a little further, Dubrov and Pushkin state:

Since, according to the non-localization principle, each element of the universe is present at any point in space (although in a form not directly observable), all a clairvoyant does is bring out, by appropriate focusing, the wave struc-

*Ibid., p. 40.

> ture of a distant object, which is latently pres-
> ent in any particular point in space.*

Don't let the term "wave structure" throw you. Basically it means that at the energetic level that underlies the
physical universe, information is simultaneously available
at all places all the time. *Now* you can be confused, if you
choose, but you will be in good company. While advanced
physicists feel they can observe this "interconnectedness"
with certainty, they, themselves, are at a loss to explain it.

What the gods of physics can't explain, we don't need to
bother our heads about. But we can observe that what we
are calling ESP and psi *can and does* exist because of this
interconnected information principle, providing, as Dubrov
and Pushkin indicate, the individual focuses on the simultaneous information available between himself and the
desired target.

It is this newly discovered universe of simultaneous information—variously being called "waves" or "energetics"—
that constitutes part of that which can be called the second
reality. Even with this minimal understanding, we can see
why *that* reality is perhaps the first reality, while the
physical-conscious reality we have been living in is the
more limited second.

In the psychic sense, what now becomes of great interest is how consciousness gets into shape to attune itself
with this vast second reality and its interconnected information. What are the central processes involved?

We will discuss these shortly. But first, if all the above
is true (and it is), then obviously a new concept of consciousness is going to have to evolve. Our awareness of
the physical universe and our thinking experience of it is
not the only form of "consciousness" we possess.

We must also have a second consciousness that integrates
with the second reality *and* with the physical as well.

*Ibid., p. 41.

In his delightful book *A New Science of Life*, Rupert Sheldrake hazards a description of this consciousness:

> Contrary to the philosophy of materialism, the conscious self can be admitted to have a reality which is not merely derivative from matter. . . . This "common sense" view leads to the conclusion that the conscious self and the body *interact*. . . . The conscious self can be thought of as interacting not with a machine, but with motor fields. The motor fields are associated with the body and depend on its physico-chemical states. But the self is neither the same as the motor fields, nor does its experience simply parallel the changes brought about within the brain by energetic and formative causation. It "enters into" the motor fields, but it remains over and above them. . . . If the conscious self has properties of its own which are not reducible to those of matter, energy, morphogenetic fields and motor fields, there is no reason why conscious memories—for example, memories of particular past events—need either be stored materially within the brain, *or* depend on morphic* resonance. They could well be given directly from past states, across time and space, simply on the basis of similarity with present states. . . .
>
> Once the conscious self is admitted to have properties unlike those of any purely physical system, it seems possible that some of these properties might be able to account for parapsychological phenomena which are inexplicable in terms of energetic or formative causation.†

---

*"Morphic" refers to the form and structure of animals and plants, while "formative" refers to results of those forms and structures.
†Rupert Sheldrake, *A New Science of Life*, J. P. Tarcher, Los Angeles, 1981, pp. 202–203.

You will note that Sheldrake is using the term "conscious self" as opposed to the term "consciousness," which normally refers only to what we are aware of while we are awake.

Sheldrake's conscious self has been referred to by other names in the past. The most traditional name, outside its theological connotations, has been, of course, soul. But it has also been called over-soul, transcendent ego, the super-self, subliminal ego, divine self, intrinsic real self, integral subconscious personality, dream self, cosmic consciousness, and as we saw in the quotation at the beginning of this chapter, Leo Talamonti, the well-known Italian parapsychologist and science popularizer, refers to it as the secret self.

Use whatever label you prefer. I've elected to use "deeper self" because it corresponds with the basic ESP core processes, which themselves lie beneath normal waking consciousness.

The capabilities of this deeper self are quite astonishing. We can by now, I think, appreciate how the deeper self participates with the interconnected information universe, the second reality. The deeper self runs on its own realities—which we might assume are in keeping with the workings of the second reality. Waking consciousness has to become "awake" to it through focusing and training. This focusing and training are not normally available in our present culture, but special education and orientation are necessary to begin to incorporate the realities of the deeper self and the second reality into one's average awareness.

It is the deeper self that is in contact with all else, albeit unknowingly to the normal consciousness. As a result, it emerges into consciousness spontaneously and even then only partly so. An example is that of telepathic bonding between loved ones: a sense of disaster, when one's kin is in danger. When Napoleon was in his first exile on the island of Elba, one day while talking to one of his generals, he suddenly began to weep for no reason that he or others could understand. It turned out that at that moment, Josephine, his first wife and love, was dying at her home outside Paris.

Dreams are our most common contact with the deeper self and its capabilities. Dream states often solve problems for us, give us glimpses of the future, predict events, link us to loved ones, and warn us of illnesses in the body before symptoms appear. Dreams have other effects that we do not readily understand, but which show the inter-connected linkage between individuals. Collective dreams have often been reported, where two people, usually linked by some special bond of affection, simultaneously dream the same event. This sharing of dreams, even if the content is not real, refutes the view that human beings can communicate only by means of language, spoken or written. At the individual level, these dreams also give credence to the concept that within the second reality, the information linkage between two people, between people and animals, or between people and a thing, can become very precise.

But we do not need to resort to dream states to begin demonstrating this linkage. We can use hard-wired ESP to begin to familiarize our conscious experience with it. After a while, the environment of this second reality will become more familiar, and many of you will begin to expand your natural ESP core to include more than just hard-wired ESP trials.

If we accept, as we now should, the existence of the second reality and a deeper self that is hooked into it, then the first issue of psychic perception revolves around those mental elements *between* the deeper self and waking consciousness that prevent the arrival of second-reality information into that consciousness.

With ample justification, we may assume the existence of a kind of psychic nucleus possessing unsuspected capabilities and powers of comprehension hidden somewhere in the recesses of the total self. With the advancing theories in quantum physics, all the evidence tells us that the rules and processes of this hidden psychic nucleus are quite unlike those of the conscious mind, and do not fit into the ordinary rational categories that characterize it. As the famous Belgian poet and dramatist Maurice Maeterlinck says in his work *L'Hote Inconnu* (The Unknown Guest): "It takes no account of time and space, those formidable yet illusory walls that prevent our reason from straying: it knows no difference of near or far, present or future, nor is it affected by the resistance of matter."

We can suppose that if there were no barriers, our everyday consciousness would be flooded with information coming into the deeper self from the second reality in which all information is interconnected. Where, in all our mental apparatus, are those barriers constructed? Many writers, such as Leo Talamonti, have suggested that the conscious mind itself, like a Freudian censor, erects these barriers in order to protect its own functions against wholesale invasion from the supersensory world of the second reality.

This may indeed be the case, at least in part. We are familiar with the fact that the conscious mind does erect barriers. We know that the conscious mind rejects almost everything that doesn't fit with its "ideal self," this phenomenon giving rise to the concept of "ego." Even when people are trying to have an "open mind" they are sometimes incapable of truly having one, especially in the face of information that contrasts too highly with their consciously held realities. In addition, many cultural and value imprints first occur in childhood, and either submerge naturally or are repressed into the unconscious where they continue to exert sway whether consciousness knows it or not.

As far as ESP is concerned, the problem is probably not that simple. It seems that, somehow, the human is constructed so that there are natural barriers between consciousness and an overwhelming influx of second-reality information. Otherwise, our consciousness would be inundated, as if listening to a thousand radio and TV channels simultaneously. We cannot imagine how we would be able to function without these natural barriers.

All the evidence suggests that these natural barriers are not irrevocably solid. Information that is meaningful to an individual often gets through. There are thousands of well-documented cases. In 1517 Pope Pius V in Rome "saw" the defeat of the Turkish fleet at Lepanto and ordered a *Te Deum* sung before receiving the official news of the victory. It is well attested (by Kant) that Emanuel Swedenborg was clearly aware of a gigantic fire destroying Stockholm hundreds of miles away. These extrasensory intrusions are especially common with sensitive mothers. On Christmas Eve, 1955, a housewife in Salerno suddenly dropped her household chores, hired a car, and drove to Teggiano in the same province. There she found her son lying dead in the gutter after a motorcycle accident. She had "seen" her son crying for help and telling her where his body could be found.

Often these extrasensory intrusions affect the individual's biosystem, although the exact information does not reach consciousness. People "feel" apprehension, which is unexplained, and only afterward find out a loved one was in danger or dying.

The greater part of spontaneous ESP that comes to be known has to do with circumstances involving a loved one. This indicates that the barriers between the second reality and consciousness *select* information that is important to the individual, and let it through the barriers. When you think of it, all this suggests some remarkable functions indeed, functions that we all must possess via the deeper self, whose nature is unfamiliar to consciousness.

We can also observe that when waking consciousness *does* try to focus on the content of extrasensory intrusions, it tends to filter the incoming information through processes that it normally uses to consciously divide information into compartments of understanding. Consciousness tends to try to make information fit into what it already knows. In this way, incoming information frequently gets distorted and misinterpreted, or it is only partially received.

The gifted psychic becomes gifted because to a large degree he or she learns intuitively to attenuate the conscious censoring processes to a point where the incoming psychic information can be more clearly perceived without being seized upon by conscious processes in which it might become misinterpreted or distorted.

In cases of powerful spontaneous ESP, this is somehow brought about naturally. The emphasis of focus shifts naturally from waking consciousness to the consciousness of the deeper self, in many cases *without* any voluntary reduction of consciousness. For the moments necessary, the deeper self assumes a greater place than does consciousness and the extrasensory experience takes place with astonishing clarity. When this happens, it is practically impossible to insist that the deeper self is unconscious, since during the course of the ESP event it is anything but unconscious.

Thus, in considering the components of the psychic nucleus, the two normal labels—consciousness and unconsciousness—are not going to stand us in very good stead. It is impossible to cram the several different components of an ESP experience into them, and it is appropriate to break down the different ESP aspects into the several components that are obviously involved.

This is best done first by giving an illustration of the entire workings.

Reading upward through this illustration, we can see that psychic information coming in from the second reality must make a path through several levels before it reaches immediate frontal consciousness.

Frontal consciousness is our everyday consciousness. It is governed solely by our senses, and its pinpoint is wher-

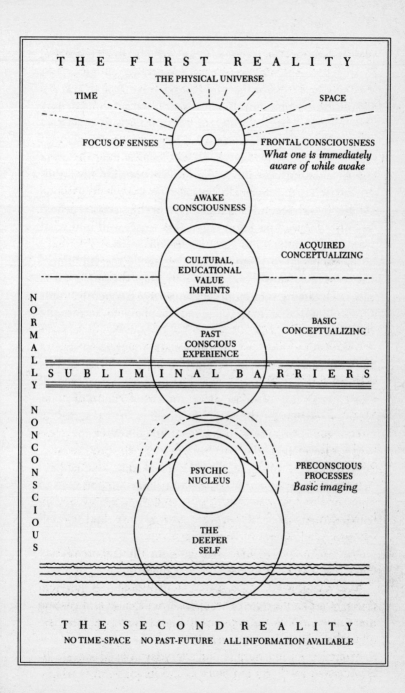

THE FIRST REALITY

THE PHYSICAL UNIVERSE

TIME

SPACE

FOCUS OF SENSES — ○ — FRONTAL CONSCIOUSNESS
What one is immediately aware of while awake

AWAKE
CONSCIOUSNESS

ACQUIRED
CONCEPTUALIZING

CULTURAL,
EDUCATIONAL
VALUE
IMPRINTS

BASIC
CONCEPTUALIZING

PAST
CONSCIOUS
EXPERIENCE

NORMALLY

SUBLIMINAL BARRIERS

NONCONSCIOUS

PSYCHIC
NUCLEUS

PRECONSCIOUS
PROCESSES
Basic imaging

THE
DEEPER
SELF

THE SECOND REALITY

NO TIME-SPACE   NO PAST-FUTURE   ALL INFORMATION AVAILABLE ever our senses are focused. When we focus on something in our past—experience or values—we temporarily can lose consciousness of the physical universe around us. We technically become unconscious of it. If we lapse too deeply into reverie, daydreaming, or reexperiencing some past experience, we can lose consciousness of being awake.

When the psychic focuses on elements or information of the psychic nucleus, he or she has to penetrate the subliminal barrier that normally acts as a dividing line between the first and second realities. His or her consciousness becomes focused on information that exists well into what we normally refer to as the unconscious.

When we go to sleep, everything above the subliminal barrier closes down, yet we know that dreaming takes place. Dreaming is often precognitive and frequently works on problems that have involved the person during the day.

When high-stage psychic information arrives in one of the consciousness areas, it does so *already* formed. This indicates that either the psychic nucleus is capable of exact perception of information and presentation of it, or that associated to the psychic nucleus are a series of preconscious processes that accomplish the work for it.

Because of this, the psychic nucleus, the preconscious processes, the subliminal barrier, and the area labeled "past conscious experience" are of primary importance to the study of new wave ESP. Taking all these together, I've labeled them the ESP core in my own work, and we will go into its elements in some detail.

We can now see that what we normally call consciousness is a matter of focus, and that focus changes depending on our interest and goals. When we deliberately try to activate an ESP experience, that consciousness can plunge its focus into the deeper self and beyond it into the elements of the second reality. When the deeper self, for reasons we do not understand, decides to send an important ESP event, it can do so of its own accord, sending upward a powerful spontaneous ESP event that can and does attenuate all the other consciousness fluctuations.

People who are already sensitive to their own psychic potentials will find this easier to grasp than those who are culturally and educationally barriered against the reality of the ESP experience. I have personally witnessed several times when trenchant disbelievers could be talked into a well-controlled ESP-viewing experiment. Many of them, to their own amazement, produced a perfectly good result. These results suggest that everyone possesses an ESP core, and that the antipsychic attitude is one that is culturally or educationally acquired.

All talents have a raw core upon which the talents rest. If the core is even partly understood, it can be built upon. Understanding, though, implies a grasp of the intrinsic nature of the core, from which one can arrive at the rules and laws at work within it and gain direction for the subsequent training, practice, and discipline needed to develop the raw core potential into a practical talent.

We are familiar with the word "core" as it applies to apples. But core means a central or foundational part of something around which other attributes are arranged. As it applies to study, the core is the arrangement of a course of studies that combines basic material from separate fields, and aims to provide a common background for all students.

Lifting the word "core" into the area of our discussion, it suggests the center or foundation of a natural talent. The source of natural talent cores is not well understood. They may be genetic, but they may also be part of one's early environment, upbringing, and education. Certain individuals seem to have a propensity for a given talent. The foundational aspect can be spotted and developed upon.

Talent cores are made up partly of intuition, partly of innate understanding, and partly of a "leaning" in the direction of a particular talent. Creativity is brought into play when one decides to develop upon the core talent. It is quite probable that talent cores are found in everyone, but are more pronounced in certain individuals. One has, so to speak, an "ear" for music, or one doesn't.

The combined work in ESP of the last fifty years suggests that almost anyone can demonstrate some minimal degree of ESP. This has led to speculation that ESP is a general but undeveloped talent in many more people than was ever thought possible. Such widespread evidence for ESP logically could not exist unless there is a natural endowment for it as part and parcel of the human makeup.

I think we will have to understand that the core itself is something quite intangible. But if it is a universal human endowment, then one should be able to elicit common, respectable effects that can be identified in anybody. Once these common core fundamentals are observed and studied, then understanding the core seems quite simple. Talent cores seem to possess a common integrity to produce similar or identical phenomena in different individuals—even in the raw state.

Once these phenomena are accepted and learned, especially in regard to their similarities—the confusion surrounding them drops away and the simplicities can be seen clearly.

There are many human talents that lie fallow until there is a need to bring them into use. There are also many natural talents that are suppressed because their exercise would conflict with prevailing values.

The study of extrasensory perception has been hindered on both counts. But times are changing; the new transformative, visionary consciousness seeks to rise above the individual, in order to comprehend the greater realities in which earth, its people, and its ecosystem exist.

△ SEVEN △

The Self-Generating Processes of the ESP Core

This book presents ESP as a natural talent. Like all the natural talents, it draws upon *all* the elements of the mind, including the brain. It transcends the limits of all these separate parts, and so is very hard to place in only one part, or even in a part of its own.

The easiest way to understand this, is to contact your own ESP core. In so doing, much of the argument about where ESP belongs quickly becomes academic.

The first step is to try a few ESP experiments that will convince you that you *can* get information about a target hidden from your sight.

You will probably be able to discriminate between your conscious efforts to "get" the information, and the information that "arrives" spontaneously in its correct or near-correct form. No amount of conscious concentration on the target will get this kind of information for you. After a dozen or more experiments, you will begin, with the help of this book, to become aware of the several phenomena closely associated with the *processes* through which you get the correct information. When you do get the target correctly, you will probably be able to see the information has arrived already processed, without any noticeable "help" from your frontal consciousness.

The term currently used to describe this "already processed" kind of phenomenon is "preconscious processing." Scientists are now beginning to understand that much of human awareness derives from preconscious processes that are hidden from the light of waking, conscious thought, and control. Core ESP clearly operates in this hidden atmosphere, and in this sense, again is comparable to other human talents.

To simplify it, I've created the following illustration, which contains the fundamentals of the ESP process as I conceive them.

There are two aspects to awareness: the conscious processes and the preconscious processes, which normally operate in nonconscious areas of the mind. Between the nonconscious and consciousness lies a band referred to as the subliminal threshold, through which incoming preconsciously processed information emerges into consciousness. Typically, the conscious mind analyzes the incoming information and tries to give it a consciously recognized structure.

If we think about this—and the fact that the ESP core can accurately construct and process psychic information— then we can understand that any impedance we may encounter, which degrades the clarity of the psychic information, comes from erroneous conscious misinterpretations of the psychic information, the misinterpretation being automatically superimposed over the true information.

Thus, we can begin to see that ESP information can be processed along at least two routes: through an unimpeded route, and through a route that passes through

THE GENERAL FLOW ROUTE OF PSYCHIC INFORMATION SHOWING SOME OF THE IMPEDANCE BARRIERS

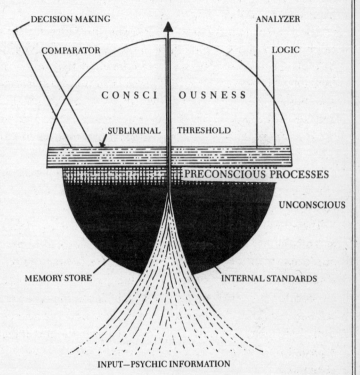

OUTPUT

DECISION MAKING

COMPARATOR

ANALYZER

LOGIC

CONSCI OUSNESS

SUBLIMINAL THRESHOLD

PRECONSCIOUS PROCESSES

UNCONSCIOUS

MEMORY STORE

INTERNAL STANDARDS

INPUT—PSYCHIC INFORMATION

NOTE:

Incoming psychic information must make its way through a veritable gauntlet of mental processes, each one being capable of impeding the clarity of the psychic information. A few are shown in the illustration above. Some are more powerful than others: *logic* or *internalized standards* can obliterate the psychic information and often do. The *comparator* compares the psychic information with past experienced information. The *compar-ator's* images often take precedence in the psy-chic's output, without the psychic's being aware that the change has occurred.

THE
UNIMPEDED ROUTE

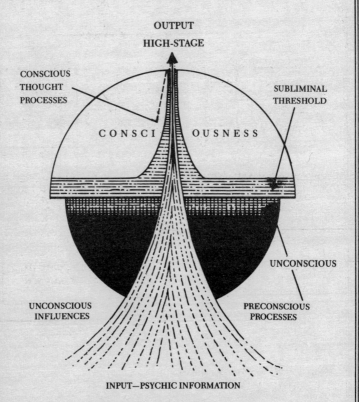

OUTPUT
HIGH-STAGE

CONSCIOUS
THOUGHT
PROCESSES

SUBLIMINAL
THRESHOLD

C O N S C I   O U S N E S S

UNCONSCIOUS

UNCONSCIOUS
INFLUENCES

PRECONSCIOUS
PROCESSES

INPUT—PSYCHIC INFORMATION

NOTE:

Incoming psychic information often makes its way
through all the mental processes that can interfere
with it without being impeded. In such cases, the
impeding mental processes either are not influ-
encing the psychic information at all, or are working in harmony with it. In cases of spontaneous
high-stage ESP, the impednce processes probably have been overthrown by unconscious factors
not yet well understood. When the individual
tries to force ESP by conscious means, the conscious mental process tends to take over and obliterate the psychic information, which is of a weaker
nature.

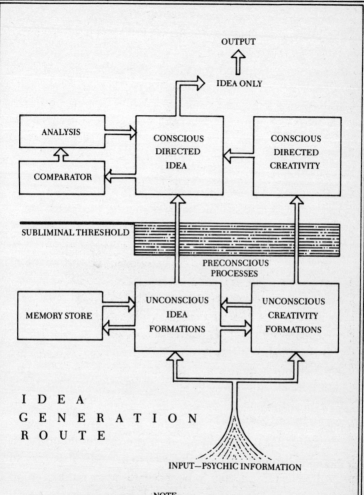

OUTPUT

IDEA ONLY

ANALYSIS

COMPARATOR

CONSCIOUS
DIRECTED
IDEA

CONSCIOUS
DIRECTED
CREATIVITY

SUBLIMINAL THRESHOLD

PRECONSCIOUS
PROCESSES

MEMORY STORE

UNCONSCIOUS
IDEA
FORMATIONS

UNCONSCIOUS
CREATIVITY
FORMATIONS

IDEA
GENERATION
ROUTE

INPUT—PSYCHIC INFORMATION

NOTE:
Anyone who has experienced idea generation and creativity
knows that they have both conscious and unconscious coun-
terparts. Extrasensory perception is not excused from these
two mysterious and powerful attributes of the human mind.
Psychic information must flow through idea-creativity formations in order to take on basic forms that can be recognizable
to logic and analysis. Many ESP results show that the psychic
information has been processed this way, and that only the
general idea of the target has resulted in the output. This
route gives the closest-to-correct result next to unimpeded
high-stage results.

conscious idea generation. The two graphics above illustrate these two routes.

The unimpeded route shows that the psychic information probably entered the mind system through some of its unconscious and unknown spectra. It passed through the preconscious processing area, where it took on form, and then was projected upward into consciousness, where it was perceived in a correct output.

The idea-forming route shows that the information was rerouted through a conscious idea generation component of the mind. When it goes through this route, the mind *adds* interpretations which are frequently incorrect.

With these routes in mind, we can quickly add another step in the overall processes which must be present in both these routes—creativity. The incoming psychic information, traveling through its preconscious processing area, where it probably gathers its general form, also must pass through a creativity process that allows the individual to participate with it in a creative sense.

It is probably at this level of interaction that the psychic information acquires a good deal of its "noise." The creativity channels are closely connected to a multitude of analytical thought processes, the emotions of the individual, and the visionary elements of his or her dreams, preoccupations, and education. If the psychic information pops up through these multifarious channels, it is easy to see how it can become impeded with other random mind elements. The following graphic shows some of the possible routes through which the psychic information can be conveyed before it reaches its final output.

I think that almost anyone who has done even a little creative work will agree that creativity and preconscious processing are very closely related. Both creative ideas and prime correct ESP information arrive out of a nebulous territory. It also seems clear that ESP is very closely associated with creativity and preconscious processing. Only

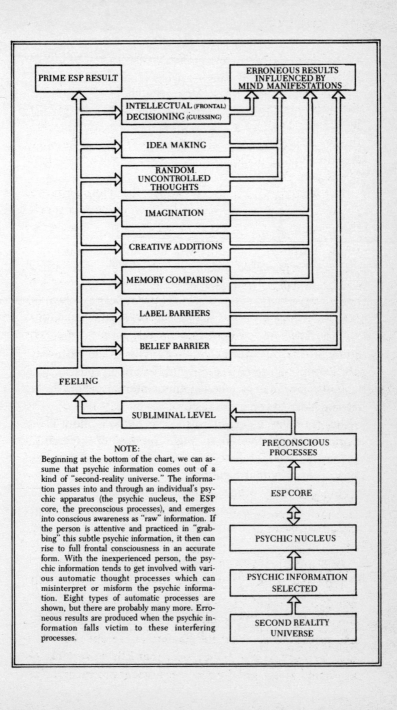

PRIME ESP RESULT

ERRONEOUS RESULTS
INFLUENCED BY
MIND MANIFESTATIONS

INTELLECTUAL (FRONTAL)
DECISIONING (GUESSING)

IDEA MAKING

RANDOM
UNCONTROLLED
THOUGHTS

IMAGINATION

CREATIVE ADDITIONS

MEMORY COMPARISON

LABEL BARRIERS

BELIEF BARRIER

FEELING

SUBLIMINAL LEVEL

PRECONSCIOUS
PROCESSES

ESP CORE

PSYCHIC NUCLEUS

PSYCHIC INFORMATION
SELECTED

SECOND REALITY
UNIVERSE

NOTE:

Beginning at the bottom of the chart, we can assume that psychic information comes out of a kind of "second-reality universe." The information passes into and through an individual's psychic apparatus (the psychic nucleus, the ESP core, the preconscious processes), and emerges into conscious awareness as "raw" information. If the person is attentive and practiced in "grabbing" this subtle psychic information, it then can rise to full frontal consciousness in an accurate form. With the inexperienced person, the psychic information tends to get involved with various automatic thought processes which can misinterpret or misform the psychic information. Eight types of automatic processes are shown, but there are probably many more. Erroneous results are produced when the psychic information falls victim to these interfering processes.

a good grasp of these processes will be what ultimately aids the neophyte who wants to develop his own ESP core.

To a large extent, creativity is self-generated in areas of the mind beyond or beneath the individual's willful, conscious control. All he can do is discipline his consciousness to accommodate the needs of the creative process. Since they seem to bear much in common at the core level, creativity, talents, and extrasensory perception are probably closely related as internal, subjective, self-generating activities beneath the level of consciousness.

If one's conscious, objective, self-willed responses work at cross-purposes, the result will be either stasis or conflict, and the impulses of talent, creativity, or extrasensory perception will be repressed or stunted.

Once the self-generated internal needs of self-generating ESP are contacted and understood, conscious ingenuity can help design better conscious environments for them in the mind. In other words, creativity, talent, and extrasensory perception can be assisted and built upon consciously, but only after the essential natural internal factors have become clear to consciousness.

The examples given in this book, showing how ESP information is delivered through the mental apparatus, demonstrate a close affinity to new models of consciousness-unconsciousness that have been arrived at by researchers in other fields. A prime example of this comes from the work done by Dr. Norman Dixon in the field of subliminal perception. One of Dixon's simpler charts is given here for comparison.

Dixon's work shows that subliminal information enters first into a nonconscious memory *store*, is processed through an *averager* and then to *internal standards*, which are probably part of the individual's nonconscious creative processes. Each of these areas involves a preconscious process of some kind.

The result of these unconscious processes rises into consciousness, where it is compared to conscious percep-

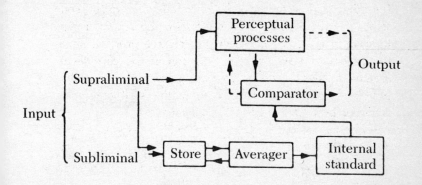

A possible model for the effect of subliminal anchors on adaptation level. The dashed lines represent the hypothesis that the subliminal anchors
affect phenomenal representation of the supraliminal series as opposed to merely affecting verbal judgments. . . . The perceptual process which
mediates all supraliminal inputs provides the other
input to the comparator. Since subliminal inputs
feed into the store, but do not activate the perceptual process directly, they influence response
only via the internal standard and comparator. If
they influence the percepts of supraliminal stim-
uli they do so indirectly by reason of their contribution to the internal standard. In so doing, of
course, their own identity is lost: they remain
effective, but subliminal. (From: Norman E.
Dixon, *Preconscious Processing*, John Wiley,
Chichester and New York, 1981, p. 25.)

tual materials. Normally the output will be an amalgam of all these. But psychic information, to be unimpeded, cannot become such an amalgam. We need to consider this when we can see that ESP is *trying* to work, but is also malfunctioning. The malfunctioning is taking place in one or more of these areas, each of which is serving to impede or degrade the accuracy of the ESP information.

To my knowledge, ESP has never been addressed as an internal *self-creating* attribute whose natural needs must be ascertained, and which must not be approached on the basis of a predetermined series of expectations. I will go farther: The cultivation of ESP is an *artistic* performance. For every art, an appropriate craft is designed, and as more is learned about the art, the craft develops accordingly. A study of the phenomena arising out of natural raw core ESP, as exemplified both in the historical examples provided in this book and in your own work, will be the beginnings of such a new craft.

△ **EIGHT** △

Picture Drawings: The First Phenomena of the ESP Core

There is an ancient enigma that people sometimes like to bother their heads with: Which
came first, the chicken or the egg?

Frontal consciousness, dealing only with physical experiences, cannot resolve this question and, in fact, can go
bonkers trying. The enigma was introduced in ancient
times as one of those intellectual exercises used to jerk the
thinking being loose from its frontal consciousness and
return it to a deeper and more basic level.

The correct answer to the chicken-egg question is not
an answer at all, but another question. When the enigma
is properly thought through, it becomes obvious that which
came first is irrelevant, since both the egg and the chicken
must have come from something else that made them both
possible in the first place. What, then, preceded the chicken
and the egg? Neither could have simply "appeared" in
completed form.

We will have better luck if we consider a similar "enigma" that is pertinent to our ESP problem. Which comes first: mental images or mental words? The reason we can have better luck is that we have individual and personal experience as well as art and science to help us out.

Children make scrawls and crude drawings long before they learn to associate words to them, and it is commonly accepted at all levels of learning that mental imaging is an inborn, natural ability. Words are acquired, although the child also possesses an inborn quality for language.

Which language the child learns is totally dependent upon the culture into which it is born, and the province or section of a country is responsible for the dialects or accents within the language. Additional languages are usually dependent upon educational opportunities.

Beneath the language system is the world of mental images, and imaging is a cross-cultural language possessed by all humans.

Basic imaging occurs long before words are learned to describe those images. Imaging, then, is closer and more intimately connected to the psychic nucleus and the ESP core.

Any information derived psychically from the second reality by the deeper self is first processed as imaging. Later in the chain of interpretation, the images are *translated* into the language the individual normally uses.

This is not to say that all languages do not exist in the general information pool the second reality represents, for there is evidence that very high-stage ESP can also process languages totally unknown to the individual. But all the evidence points to the fact that when you are first trying to contact your own basic ESP core, it is more progressive to undercut the difficulties imposed by languaging, and allow the basic imaging processes to provide the first and most natural work.

As I mentioned earlier, parapsychology is a highly *verbalized* science. While many of the targets parapsy-

chologists use are in pictorial form, the subjects' responses
are normally given in a *language* form. Subjects are asked
to describe in words what they are "seeing." They are
hardly ever asked to *draw* their responses. This is standard procedure in parapsychology, but most of the researchers cannot see that it forces the subjects to doubly
process the psychic information they are getting. Once the
basic image-laden psychic information leaves the psychic
nucleus and is forced into the conscious or semiconscious
processes of wording, the mind enters into the response.
A great deal of distortion and misrepresentation can and
does take place while the mind seeks to translate the basic
images into words.

The well-developed psychic intuitively learns to release
conscious wording in favor of perceiving basic images.
With experience, the mind will learn how to integrate
ESP information into its workings, and then wording will
become easier. But if the basic imaging nature of the
psychic is dropped out or ignored, as is so frequently the
case, the individual will have a very difficult time in
adequately experiencing ESP at its most basic level.

Let's take a hypothetical example. A friend of a rather
elegant woman places an object on a table in another
room. The elegant woman, after quibbling that she can't
draw at all, nevertheless is coaxed into trying to use her
ESP core to perceive what the unknown object is. She
produces the following small sketch:

She was surprised that this sketch emerged from her almost automatically. When asked what the sketch represents, she first says that there was something slimy about it, but that it could be a vase, but on the other hand, it might be a pitcher, a jar, a can, a water jug, and so forth. Wording has given her many possibilities. When shown the target, it turns out to be a used can of motor oil. She looks at it, and says, "Well, I'm totally unfamiliar with those things." Yet her psychic nucleus had automatically given her the correct shape, and also had produced a feeling of sliminess.

The most correct portions of her response were achieved without any conscious processes. When these were invoked by asking her what the drawing represented, the response departed from accuracy and became misrepresented.

Many adults will say that they cannot draw, forgetting that as children they were busy drawing images, probably long before they could talk fluently. The innate ability and desire to externalize images is very important as a whole and, as we now see, of primary importance to the essential, basic ESP experience.

Some of the most convincing examples of ESP come from developed psychics who, after learning to have confidence in their drawings, have produced astonishing evidence, both for ESP *and* for the value of picture drawings. For instance, the famous Mexican psychic, Maria Reyes de Z., was once handed a nondescript piece of marble. She executed the following sketch:

This particular experiment—and there are hundreds of other examples—very well substantiates the new hypotheses in physics—that in the second reality, all information is available in some sort of perpetual wave form. All a developed psychic needs is a point of focus, at which time, if all other things go well, he or she can attune to the information. The next step is to let the psychic nucleus do the work it is cut out to do *without* involving it in the

The piece of marble was from the Roman Forum. Below is a photograph of it as it appeared at the time of the experiment.

misinterpretations that can occur in conscious manipulation of incoming psychic information.

The fundamental point to be drawn is that there exists in all of us a basic, but undeveloped, function. Our ESP core works automatically, if we can but learn to allow it to do so. Furthermore, from the picture drawings, we can perceive how well the ESP core is working, and by careful observation of the picture drawings themselves, learn from them.

The Search for Picture Drawings

As a result of my own first picture drawings in 1971, I began a search to locate other examples of picture drawings. My purpose was twofold. I wanted to have some idea of individuals in the past who had demonstrated ESP through picture drawings. I felt it was important to know a little bit about what kind of people they had been. I wanted to know if they had any special characteristics that might serve as a role model in my own attempts to further develop my own ESP.

It is a common expectation to think there must be something special about a person who is psychic. A truly developed psychic does become special, but for the most part, all the individuals who had produced picture drawings were what we would call quite ordinary people. Their ordinariness eventually impressed me very much. They had chanced upon their psychic ability, demonstrated it to researchers, and then apparently went back into their ordinary lives. Hardly any of them became a great, developed psychic. They remain generally unknown, save for the initials by which they were identified in research reports.

This factor made me think that perhaps psychical research and parapsychology are, unknowingly, involved with two very different types of ESP. The testing of great and

famous psychics is acknowledged; but what about the startling ESP that has come from ordinary people? Those who
had no clue that they could be psychic, yet inadvertently
tripped across it in themselves? Surely this group constitutes something different from, say, the naturally psychically aware individual who consciously develops his or her
abilities.

Because of this factor, I have, through the years, always
been very interested in watching someone who has never
had a psychic experience attempt a picture drawing experiment. Many of these people insist they are not, and could
not be, psychic. Yet to their surprise, they have frequently produced results that astonish themselves.

The second purpose of my search for picture drawings
developed out of the first one. When I began to compare
the picture drawings, one of the first things that became
apparent was that there were too many similarities among
them. The first similarity was that aside from a few minor
stylistic forms, it would be easy enough to think that the
same person had drawn them all. When the individual did
not get the target correctly, or only partially so, the dis-
crepancies were generally portrayed in much the same
way.

Sets of picture drawings achieved in the 1880s can be
compared with sets obtained in the 1970s (and with all
those in the intervening years), and the different characteristics are all similar. You can virtually see the difficulties the psychic nucleus is having as it tries to push the
psychic information into consciousness. The difficulties
are, in fact, identical.

Comparison and observation of these difficulties eventually made it possible to construct a list of some different
types of interferences that can be experienced as one tries
to execute a picture drawing. Examples will be given in
some detail later in this book.

Starting with a high-stage result in which the picture
drawing is a more or less exact rendering of the target, the

variances cover a gamut of interference patterns, right down to the lowest-stage result possible—no correspondence to the target at all.

Some of these difficulties apparently take place in the raw inexperienced ESP core itself; but far more of them can obviously be attributed to interference by consciousness as it tries to relate the incoming psychic information to elements of experience it already contains. If the conscious mind tries to dominate the incoming psychic information, it can obliterate it.

The most wonderful thing about all this is that we know that consciousness can learn *if* it can be made to understand exactly what it is supposed to learn. After I had memorized the list of types of interference, my mind mound ESP system collaborated much better with the basic elements of the psychic nucleus and its ESP core. The mind manifestations of the consciousness functions either withdrew completely, letting unhampered ESP information through, or began to work in harmony with it. As a result, I began to be able to produce under testing, psychic information of some importance.

To illuminate the examples I've chosen for this book (only a few out of the two hundred or so available), it is of human interest to know a little bit about the people who produced them. There are nine major sets of examples in existence where we have a large collection of picture drawings taken from a small number of people. Beyond that, there are many more examples, but from people who produced only a few, and in some cases only one or two. The sources in which the major sets can be found are given at the front of the bibliography.

People Who Have Produced Picture Drawings

The first picture drawings achieved were produced by George Albert Smith during the winter of 1882 and 1883 at the Society for Psychical Research in London, not long after its founding. The picture drawings were so startling and accurate that they were hotly contested by critics, and the first large scandal in the history of organized psychic research erupted in full flames.

In its day and time, the scandal was long and horrendous. It revolved around whether or not Smith and his associate, one Douglas Blackburn, could have cheated and fooled the early eminent psychical researchers whose scientific reputations were at stake. In 1888, one of the two major researchers involved died in completely mysterious circumstances suggesting suicide because of the possibility that Smith had cheated. This scandal has never really been put to rest, and critics continue to cull the events hoping to find final evidence.

Smith's story is worth relating for two reasons. The scandal cast a pall over picture drawings in general and is probably one of the reasons many subsequent researchers shied away from them. But Smith's picture drawings, compared to other examples that have accumulated through the years, show that they exhibit all the important characteristics of the psychic picture drawing processes which are identical in *all cases*. Smith could hardly have prefabricated his picture drawings to match the qualities of others that had not even come into being. This retrospective evidence shows that Smith did not cheat, and that his work should be resurrected for what it is—an example of prime and accurate psychic functioning.

Douglas Blackburn was born in 1857 in the district of Southwark in London. By the time he was twenty-three (in 1880), he was the editor of a small journal (*The Brightonian*) published in Brighton.

His writings in *The Brightonian* made it clear that he was deeply interested in the world of entertainment, especially in conjuring performances and in the public exposure of the fallacies of spiritualism, and in exposing mediums and second-sight or mind-reading acts.

In *The Brightonian* of April 22, 1882, Douglas Blackburn began to publish a series of extremely complimen-
tary reports on the public performances of a stage mesmerist,
a local youth named George Albert Smith. Smith had
been born in 1864 of humble parents in the Cripplegate
district of East London. Smith was earning his livelihood
as a local seaside entertainer, and had a wide knowledge
of conjuring and a considerable ingenuity in the invention
of new tricks.

What the exact relationship between Blackburn and
Smith was is avoided in the available literature, but Blackburn clearly went beyond any normal duty as a journalist
in heaping praise upon the stage presentations of the
younger Smith. By September 1882, the two were working together giving paid public entertainments in pseudo–
thought transference.*

It was Blackburn who contacted researchers in the newly
formed Psychical Research Society, and it was under their
auspices that the notorious experiments took place.

The two principal researchers that conducted the Smith-
Blackburn experiments were Mr. Frederick W. H. Myers
(1834–1901) and Mr. Edmund Gurney (1847–1888).

Frederick Myers was a profound scholar, a poet of
distinction, and a brilliant psychologist. For thirty years he
filled the post of inspector of schools at Cambridge, from
which he resigned to pursue psychical investigations. He
wrote several books, and of the sixteen volumes of
proceedings of the Psychical Research Society published
while he lived, there was not one without an important
contribution from his pen.

Edmund Gurney was a distinguished English psychical
researcher, whose many works were among the mainstays
of the Psychical Research Society. It was the discovery of
thought transference which aroused his enduring interest
in psychical research. Between 1885 and 1888 he devised

---

*"Thought transference" was the term commonly used immediately before
the term "telepathy" was coined.

a large number of experiments by which he proved that there is sometimes, in the induction of hypnotic phenomena, some agency at work which is neither ordinary nervous stimulation, nor suggestion conveyed by any ordinary channel to the subject's mind.

When, under the auspices of Gurney and Myers, Smith and Blackburn began their demonstrations, the two men were allowed to hold each other's hands. This was not then an unusual method. Mind or thought reading had progressed along these lines for some time. The results from these first experiments can well be disregarded.

Later on, Blackburn, who fixed the selected targets in his mind for Smith to try to perceive, was in another room, with Gurney and Myers keeping careful watch to prevent deliberate communication between them. At this point, Smith had started *drawing* what he felt he was getting. It is these drawings that demonstrate what was, by comparison to subsequent experiments of the same kind, his core ESP potential.

The first reports published about thought transference created a considerable stir in England, and interest in picture drawings spread to the Continent. This was a time long before radio and TV, and households were used to finding ways to entertain themselves. It wasn't long before thought transference and picture drawings became the rage in parlor games and at parties. Many wonderful examples of core ESP appear to have been produced at this level, but only a very few remain in existence today.

A few of these examples came to the attention of the Society of Psychical Research, and when the results bore up under extremely good testing controls, they were published by the society.

Another interesting case of early picture drawing concerned Mr. Malcolm Guthrie, a partner in the leading drapery sales firm of Liverpool. He was also a city magistrate and a student of philosophy.

In 1883 two saleswomen, Miss Edwards and Miss Relph,

worked in his drapery showroom. We know little more about the women than their names. We can only presume they were quite ordinary, and had taken an interest in trying to send psychic information to each other. Their results were very good, and when Guthrie learned of their psychic work, he took an interest in helping them design their experiments so that they could withstand all possible criticism. He invited James Birchall, the honorable secretary of the Liverpool Literary and Philosophical Society, to act as an independent observer and watchdog of the experiments.

Miss Edwards and Miss Relph lived and worked under circumstances entirely different from Douglas Blackburn and George Albert Smith, yet the results of their core ESP are almost identical to those obtained from Smith.

Almost immediately on the heels of the Edwards-Relph experiments came demonstrations of picture drawing by a very young Kate Smith, who began experiments with her older brother Mr. J. W. Smith (not to be confused with G. A. Smith) of Brunswick Place, Leeds. Not much biographical information is available on these two, but the archives indicate that J. Smith was a "highly intelligent young man, quite alive to the precautions to be taken to avoid obvious errors in experiment."

Sir William Fletcher Barrett interviewed this brother-sister team himself. Barrett was a professor of physics at the Royal College of Science (from 1873 to 1910) at Dublin and was one of the early, but very distinguished, psychical researchers. He was the secretary of the British Society for Psychical Research, and under his auspices Kate Smith was tested. Her picture drawings bear remarkable resemblance to those of G. A. Smith and Miss Edwards and Miss Relph.

These first picture drawing experiments made a terrific impact on science and public alike. The rage for attempting thought transference and picture drawings spread to Berlin and Paris, and to the United States. In the United

States the climate for ESP was so scientifically forbidding that the vogue was not supported by any scientific interest.

In 1886, the famous German philosopher and researcher into the problems of aesthetics, Max Dessoir, began experimenting with picture drawing experiments. Max Dessoir was unusual in the field of parapsychology, because he studied parapsychological phenomena not from the strict scientific viewpoint, but from that of aesthetics; that is, as phenomena akin to those of art. His writings on psychic phenomena (most not translated into English) are a valuable asset for anyone wanting to comprehend the intricacies of the ESP core, because he compares them to the problems of creativity.

Herr Dessoir sent one contribution on thought transference to the SPR in England, who published it in 1888. It is a small contribution, but one that further confirms the startling accuracy of core ESP.

Max Dessoir might have contributed much more to our understanding of psychic phenomena than he was allowed to. He was an early casualty of the Nazis.

One of Dessoir's picture drawers was Frau von Goeler-Ravensburg, who focused on drawings being made in another room. She then drew her impressions, which turned out to be exact representations of the targets.

At the same time as the Dessoir experiments, 1886 and 1887, the most massive of the early picture drawing experiments was taking place in Paris. Monsieur A. Schmoll experimented with his family and friends and a Monsieur J. E. Maibre. The details of these experiments might have been lost had they not finally been published by the British society in 1888. They represent a tour de force that reveals many different types of problems that will be encountered in attempting picture drawings.

Schmoll's group consisted of the following people: Mme D., aged 45, who was not generally successful in the reproduction of picture drawings; Mlle Marthe D., aged 22, who showed little interest; Mlle Jane D., aged 22, who was healthy though had a delicate constitution, but who exhibited a very decided faculty for the psychic perception of hidden objects, and in reproducing them through picture drawings; Mlle Eugenie P., an artist, aged 30, subject to headaches, but who provided a good number of satisfactory results; Mlle Louis M., 26, who gave good results, but left the experiments due to ill health; M. E.S., aged 30, a political writer, strong and vigorous, who was employed only as a sender of psychic information; and Madame Schmoll, M. Schmoll, and M. Maibre.

Not much more biological information is available, save for the fact that Schmoll was interested in hypnotism and compared the picture drawer's psychic state to lucid states observed during hypnosis. None of these individuals was a developed psychic, yet their collective picture drawings display an extremely wide diversity of the processes involved as the ESP core goes about its work.

Meanwhile, the publication of all these early successful picture drawings (and their implications) had outraged skeptical scientists of the time. Attacks on the validity of the experiments became commonplace, as did attacks on the major researchers themselves. Their qualifications as researchers were questioned, and at times their sanity also.

In 1890 in Berlin a certain odious Albert Moll published a book entitled *Hypnotism,* with an English version coming out later the same year. Moll presented what was to become the standard antipsychic strategy for debunking the phenomena of core ESP, which by now had begun to be referred to as the "higher phenomena." Moll insisted that it could probably be proved that the results obtained could always be accounted for by hyperacuity of the normal senses. In other words, a natural explanation could always be found, and that controls established by researchers to exclude some kind of sensory cueing were always inefficient. He had found only one series of experiments in which the controls could not be faulted, those of

Malcolm Guthrie. Moll's will to disbelieve was confessed by himself, in concluding his criticisms of Malcolm Guthrie's experiments. But unable to fault them, he nonetheless said that he was "subjectively convinced that some sources of error were overlooked, and that suggestion was somehow or other called into play."

This tactic has been used ever since to dumbfound all successful parapsychology. No matter how convincingly and well-controlled any experiment is, the critics frequently still rave that the researchers must have overlooked something that would allow the experiment to be explained in normal, nonpsychic, terms. And when the controls of the experiment cannot be faulted, the clear thinking of the researchers can be brought into question.

As the first president of the Society for Psychical Research, Henry Sidgwick, observed as early as 1883: "All records of experiments must depend ultimately on the probity and intelligence of the persons recording them, and it is impossible for us, or any other investigators, to demonstrate to persons who do not know us that we are not idiotically careless or consciously mendacious." This issue is further confounded by critics who insist that when researchers can prove they are not consciously cheating, they may be guilty of some unconscious cheating that even they are not aware of.

Brian Inglis notes:

> Inevitably, to convince skeptical academics that psychical research was "clean" the researchers had to introduce controls of a rigour which no other academic discipline was asked to accept; controls designed to ensure not simply that subjects could not cheat, but also that the investigators themselves could not cheat. It proved a futile enterprise. People in strait-jackets are taken to be crazy.*

*Brian Inglis, *Science and Parascience: A History of the Paranormal, 1914–1939*, Hodder and Stoughton, London, 1984, p. 341.

Today, it is a well-understood tactic of mind manipulation that if an unknown and unresolvable guilt can be established among a group of people (such as parapsychologists represent), that group can be controlled and subdued. As long as the target group accepts the possibility that the guilt might be true in some ways, it remains introverted and creatively unproductive. All its resources go into trying to resolve the "guilt" that does not exist in the first place. As already mentioned, Moll first enunciated this tactic, and it is used to this day.

The onus of proof lies with parapsychologists, but only to the degree science normally requires. They need not go beyond that and prove themselves also. The onus of disproof lies with critics. As Inglis points out, "Where sceptics have too often erred in the past is in criticizing the evidence second-hand, as it were, often on the basis of earlier, and also second-hand, criticism, without going back to the original source material. It is still there, in abundance."*

In the case of proving picture drawings, the work is not the privileged domain only of psychical researchers. Picture drawings are easy to obtain. All one needs is two trusting people with a wall between them and the target. Critics and skeptics can set up this simple experiment themselves. Assuming that their own honesty, conscious or otherwise, is beyond dispute, some of them doubtlessly will achieve an activation of their own ESP cores.

Altogether, this patently unfair critical approach, coupled with the enormous scandal about George Albert Smith, brought about a state of affairs in which many subsequent researchers turned away from picture drawing experiments. But the experiments did not cease by any means and, in fact, became more revelatory as time passed.

On January 15, 1890, in Munich, the Baron Albert von Schrenck-Notzing (1862–1929) began a series of thought

*Ibid., p. 15.

transference experiments with a young man referred to in the literature only as Graf S. (aged 20) and a young woman, Fraulein A. No other biological details of the two picture drawers are available. Dr. Schrenck-Notzing, however, was a German pioneer in psychical research, as well as a physician in Munich who specialized in psychiatry. He was one of the most productive of all the famous early psychical researchers, although his work has been eclipsed by other lesser but more popular researchers; and because much of his work has never been translated into English.

Schrenck-Notzing's gatherings of evidence were enormous, and he investigated and worked with some of the most famous of the European psychics and mediums. For our purposes of revealed core ESP, we will use samples from his work with Graf S. and Fraulein A.

The early picture drawing manifestations that reflected excellent core ESP faded into oblivion during WWI.

In 1925, picture drawing core ESP again emerged through the experiments associated with René Warcollier (1881–1962). Out of these early efforts, Warcollier eventually published a book in which the various elements of core ESP are clearly set out.

Warcollier was a chemical engineer and an author, who became interested in the paranormal. In addition to his work as a chemical engineer, he studied the nature of telepathy (formerly called thought transmission) and he collaborated in experiments with the noted Eugene Osty and Cesar de Vesme. Between 1951 and 1962 he was president of the *Institut Metapsychique International* in Paris, for which he acted as editor of their journal, the *Revue Metapsychique*.

Overall, the work of Warcollier is of paramount importance because he readopted the technique of sketching out psychically received information.

In 1928, a very significant contribution, again reaffirming picture drawings, was made in the United States and from what appeared to be a very unlikely source.

At first sight, Upton Sinclair seems to have been the type of person who might be expected to reject ESP and its implications. Living between 1878 and 1968, he produced more than eighty books, with underlying themes of social and industrial reform. He was a socialist, and his novel *The Jungle* (1906), a brutally graphic novel of the Chicago stockyards, aroused great public indignation and led to reform of federal food inspection laws. He established a short-lived socialist community, Helicon Home Colony. He was defeated as the Democratic candidate for governor of California in 1934.

Among his other novels exposing social evils are *King Coal* (1917), *Oil!* (1927), *Boston* (on the Sacco-Vanzetti Case, 1928), and *Little Steel* (1938). His social studies include *The Brass Check* (1919) and *The Goose-Step* (1923). His novel *Dragon's Teeth* (1942) won him a Pulitzer prize.

Upton Sinclair's interest in ESP is perhaps surprising, since the strong materialistic substructure that lies under most concepts of socialism seems to oblige socialists to reject nonmaterial phenomena out of hand and without inspection of facts.

Mr. Sinclair's outlook is well stated in his book *Mental Radio*, which is a recounting of the experiments that involved his wife, Mary Craig Sinclair.

> I began reading books on psychic research. From first to last, I have read hundreds of volumes; always interested, and always uncertain—an uncomfortable mental state. The evidence in support of telepathy came to seem to me conclusive, yet it never quite became real to me. The consequences of belief would be so tremendous, the changes it would make in my view of the universe so revolutionary, that I didn't believe, even when I said I did.
>
> But for thirty years the subject has been among the things I hoped to know about; and, as it

happened, fate was planning to favour me. It
sent me a wife who became interested, and
who not merely investigated telepathy, but
learned to practice it. For the past three years I
have been watching this work, day by day, and
night by night, in our home. So at last I can say
that I am no longer guessing. Now I really
know. I am going to tell you about it, and hope
to convince you; but regardless of what anybody can say, there will never again be a doubt
about it in my mind. I KNOW!*

The interested reader will, of course, like to track down
a copy of the Sinclairs' book which contains hundreds of
examples of picture drawings. In those cases where a
picture drawing was produced, of course, the core ESP
elements stand forth for what they are.

For the most part, Mary Craig Sinclair worked with a
man named Bob Irwin, who created the drawings she
tried to duplicate by ESP. Later, Mr. Sinclair created
drawings for her.

Mary Craig always sat in another room behind a closed
door; but as Sinclair points out, because some of the
experiments were done with many miles between, "you
may verify [yourself] my assertion that the telepathic
[information] energy, whatever it may be, knows no difference between thirty feet and forty miles. The results
with Bob and with myself were about the same."

Even though *Mental Radio* arrived in American consciousness more or less as a bombshell, its implications
did not catch on. It is generally conceded that the book
brought public support to ESP, but it was avoided by the
formal scientific research groups in the United States.

There is hardly any evidence that anyone else attempted
picture drawings. The picture drawing technique did not

*Upton Sinclair, *Mental Radio*, Werner Laurie, London, 1930, p. 10.

reemerge until 1971 when I inadvertently caused it to be incorporated into the OOB experiments at the ASPR.

When I was invited in late 1972 to take part in preliminary experiments at the Stanford Research Institute (now SRI International), I had already made my first assessment of the primal importance of the picture drawing technique. When I joined the project at SRI International in 1973, one of my first contributions to that project was a stressing of the importance of picture drawings. As a result of my emphatic urging and the evidence I was able to provide, the picture drawing method of collecting ESP responses was adopted by the workers at SRI International, even though the verbal method of collecting data continued to be used also.

All things considered, it has been the proliferation of successful picture drawings that has catapulted the work at SRI International into worldwide prominence.

The project was headed by Harold E. Puthoff until August 1985, at which time he accepted a position at the Institute for Advanced Studies at Austin. With a rare combination of courage and tenacity, he kept his project on track through stressful times. Puthoff was born in Chicago in 1936, achieved his doctorate in electrical engineering from Stanford University, and supervised research for Ph.D. candidates in electrical engineering and applied physics at Stanford University. He was responsible for developing a tunable Raman laser producing high-power radiation throughout the infrared section of the spectrum, and is co-author of a standard textbook on lasers. It has been my pleasure to have had a working relationship with him in the field of psychoenergetics, and to have been his colleague in many of the problematical aspects presented by psychic phenomena.

The psychoenergetic project at SRI is best known for having developed experiments into remote viewing. Remote viewing is an amalgam of what used to be called thought transference, telepathy, and clairvoyance. It is a process whereby a viewer (formerly the subject or the sensitive) perceives information about a distant location and tries to describe the location, often in great detail, before the location is known to him.

The results of these experiments demonstrate raw core ESP, often almost identical to the historic work we have discussed. The remote viewing work owes its robust characteristics primarily to two factors. The first is the return to the picture drawing techniques. The second is the participation of people from all walks of life, who to a large extent have been successful. The untapped pool of psychic giftedness has once again been tapped, demonstrating the prevalence of its existence in the spectrum of human talents.

The experimental design emanating from the psychoenergetics project at SRI has been copied all over the world, so that similar results have been achieved by researchers independent of the SRI environment.

With a few exceptions, almost all the work at SRI has been produced by individuals who were trying remote viewing for the first time. Very few of them were self-achieved psychics. Just ordinary people. These examples were achieved by a variety of methods. Some represent objects hidden in cans, or in another room. Some represent instances where one person went to a place unknown to the viewer and then the viewer, at a prearranged time, tried to describe (and draw) the place. One or two examples have used geographic coordinates only to specify a far distant site totally unknown to the viewer.

The examples of SRI picture drawings incorporated in this book are some of those achieved by myself and by Hella Hammid. When Hammid first volunteered for experiments at SRI, she was unfamiliar with her own ESP. She is an extremely cultured woman of Austrian origin and a photographer of renown. When she first set pencil to paper to record her ESP impressions, her core performed as well as her predecessors', and in some cases even better.

The purpose of this brief history has been to bring out the fact that a picture drawing core ESP has been demonstrated by individuals from all walks of life. The thing that unites these individuals is the fact that they all attempted to record their ESP impressions via a picture drawing. From their so doing, three factors can now be ascertained:

• We are justified in thinking that an ESP core exists in all individuals.

• The picture drawing method actually obtains more precise information about a hidden target than does the wording method, which is fraught with inaccuracies and misinterpretation.

• By comparing the bulk of picture drawings, we can begin to categorize the preconscious processes that are taking place, and learn to improve our conscious reception of ESP information by observing the apparent difficulties the information undergoes as it tries to reach consciousness.

△ **NINE** △

Remarkable Picture Drawings

At this point, let me show you two kinds of phenomena that can be produced by the ESP core.

In the first set of the examples given below (Illustrations 1–9), the subject's ESP core functioned in an unimpeded manner, and the actual elements of the target were more or less correctly perceived.

In the second set (Illustrations 10–18), the core was apparently impeded somewhat so that all the subject got was the general idea of what the target represented.

The wide difference between the apparent functions of the ESP core might not at first be visible. Both these sets would be accepted as "hits" in any parapsychology experiment. But actually, whereas the first set represents the core working unimpeded, the second set shows that the ESP information has been taken over by consciousness, which, in turn, is projecting only an intellectual idea about the target, albeit a correct idea. But in the second set, we are no longer in direct hard-wired contact with the target, but are viewing a mind manifestation of it. The mind manifestation has modified the actual target a bit, and is trying to turn the response into wording based upon an idea that corresponds to something in conscious experience.

A dynamic shift of focus in the central process has taken place. The focus has left the psychic information itself, and turned into a focus somewhere in the mind, which is attempting to correlate the information with something known.

This is one of the first dynamic shifts each of you will encounter when you design your own experiments.

Each of the two sets given below are from nine different individuals, and span one hundred years. Yet you will be able to note that they all have a great similarity, not only in the execution of the drawing itself, but in the difficulties the individuals encountered with their ideas in the second set.

Before you review these historical examples, let me say that I believe I have confirmed that they were all achieved under unimpeachable experimental conditions. What will be most important is that when you try your own experiments, you will find out how easy it is. Many of you will enjoy focusing on your own ESP core and producing results that are similar to those given here.

What we are after is an activation of the ESP core in you. It is only through this method that a new age in ESP can emerge where it belongs—in the hands of the people who are courageous enough to take the plunge.

Illustration 1

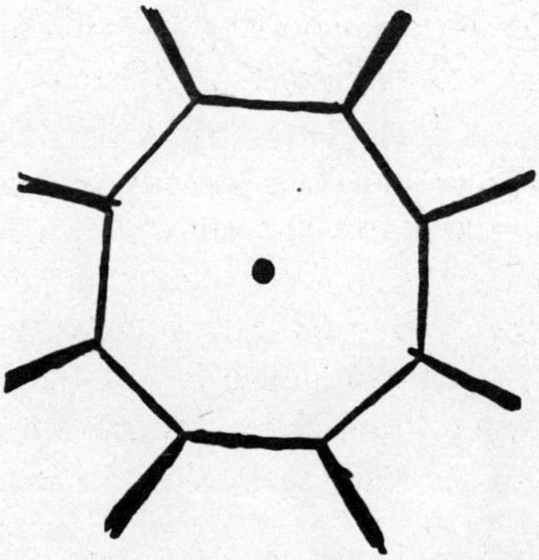

TARGET

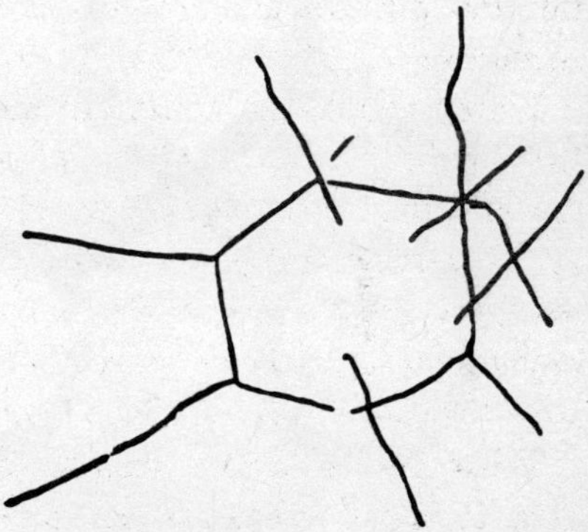

RESPONSE

George Albert Smith (1882)

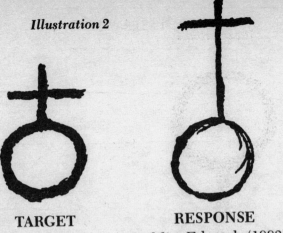

Illustration 2

TARGET

RESPONSE
Miss Edwards (1883)

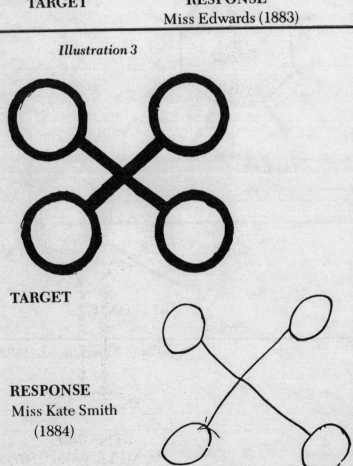

Illustration 3

TARGET

RESPONSE
Miss Kate Smith
(1884)

Illustration 4

TARGET

RESPONSE
M. Maibre series (1887)

Illustration 5

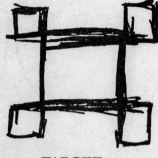

TARGET

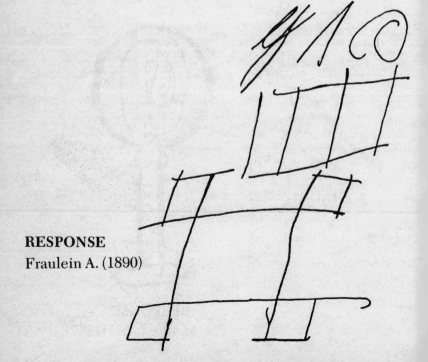

RESPONSE
Fraulein A. (1890)

Illustration 6

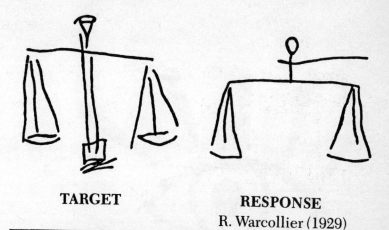

TARGET

RESPONSE
R. Warcollier (1929)

Illustration 7

TARGET

RESPONSE
Mary Craig Sinclair (1929)

Illustration 8

TARGET

RESPONSE
Ingo Swann (1973)

Illustration 9

TARGET
Leather Belt Keyring

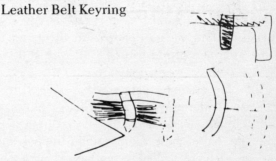

RESPONSE

"The strongest image
I get is like a belt."

Hella Hammid (1979)

Looking over the foregoing nine illustrations, you will
have noted that the target and the subjects' response were
almost identical. You must bear in mind that these spec-
tacular results were achieved when the target was hidden
from the subjects' senses, that they were achieved by
extrasensory means only.

You might also have concluded, considering the accuracy
of these results, that the subjects were highly developed or

talented psychics. This is not the case at all. Each of the nine subjects was inexperienced in performing psychic feats. The remarkable results achieved show that in each of them there exists a psychic nucleus and ESP core which, in the case of each of the examples given, worked naturally to produce the result.

The natural ESP core, however, does not always work with this kind of excellence. Other mental imaging functions of the individual's consciousness can get in the way of a pure psychical perception of a given talent and degrade its accuracy. Unless such interference is located, understood, and overcome, no suitable training can take place. In fact, understanding the sources of ESP degradation is probably the first step to take in any ESP training course. Before we go deeper into them, let us look at some examples of the natural ESP core still functioning, but not with complete accuracy.

The nine examples below were rendered by the same individuals who provided the earlier examples, under the same circumstances, and in the same time periods. You will note that in these additional illustrations, the subjects did not accurately identify the target, but achieved only the general *idea* of what the target was.

Illustration 10

TARGET

RESPONSE
George Albert Smith (1882)

Illustration 11

TARGET

RESPONSE
Miss Edwards
(1883)

Illustration 12

RESPONSE
Miss Kate Smith
(1884)

TARGET

Illustration 13

TARGET

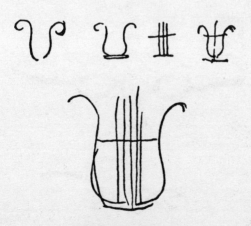

RESPONSE

M. Maibre series (1887)

Illustration 14

TARGET

RESPONSE
Fraulein A. (1890)

Illustration 15

TARGET

RESPONSE
R. Warcollier (1929)

Illustration 16

RESPONSE

(In this case, the general idea of the target was converted by the ESP system into words.)

Mary Craig Sinclair (1929)

TARGET

Illustration 17

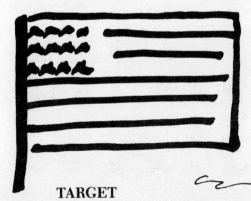

TARGET

RESPONSE

(General idea as a sketch, converting immediately into words.)

Ingo Swann (1973)

Illustration 18

TARGET
Curled-up leaf

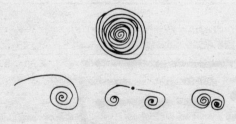

RESPONSE
A nautilus shape with a tail

Hella Hammid (1977)

In Illustrations 10–18, the incoming psychic signals about the target are being processed through an additional channel, and impeded, through the ESP core. Incoming psychic signals are processed through several mental layers which tend to degrade the accuracy of prime or high-stage extrasensory perception. This impedance can become so gross as to ultimately leave no observable correspondence between the target material and the subject's response. Even though each of these nine people did produce the high-stage accurate renderings, they did so only once in a while. Many times they failed completely to identify the target.

From all this it is possible to see that the raw ESP core, though capable of spontaneous high-stage, accurate ESP, is nevertheless subject to other mental functions. The individual's mental patterns often intrude, using plain guessing as to what the target might be, usually to the degree that the psychic information trying to come in through the prime ESP core cannot reach active consciousness. So the subject identifies not the target, but extraneous elements "going on in his head." This adverse phenomenon is referred to in modern parapsychology as "noise," and is analogous to static on a radio frequency. The comparison is very apt. It's actually like several radio signals converging over the same frequency, entirely blotting out the channel one wants to hear.

For the individual who earnestly wishes to develop his ESP potential, this "noise" presents profound difficulties. But learning about it, especially through the literature, is an important step toward perfecting your own ESP potential.

Rather than ending this chapter on the dour note of ESP noise, let us restore our hopes a little by looking at three examples of unimpeded, or nearly unimpeded, raw core ESP with targets that are (my experience can vouch for it) very, very difficult—alphabet letters. The alphabet letters A, B and A B C were used as targets in Illustrations 19–21. The prime unimpeded ESP core processed the accurate information clearly.

Each of these "alphabet" attempts verify one of the difficult phenomena of the ESP core. In each case, the subject had no idea the target would be alphabet letters. When the psychic signals started coming in through the ESP core, they appear to have come in as bits and pieces. This was noted in Smith's early drawing; the experimentor noted that it was as if "the mental picture were 'glimpsed' piecemeal."

Illustration 19

TARGET

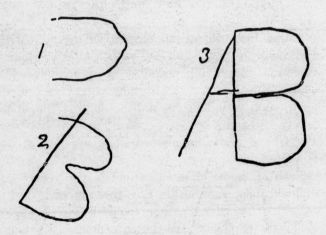

RESPONSE

George Albert Smith (1882)

Illustration 20

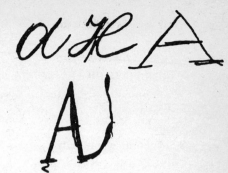

TARGET

RESPONSE
Fraulein A. (1890)

Illustration 21

TARGET

this must be letters

RESPONSE
Ingo Swann (1973)

You will note that with his combined alphabet target (Illustration 19) George Albert Smith had to make more than one attempt to realize the AB relationship. Finally he did so quite excellently (nearly unbelievably so at the time).

Several years later, Fraulein A. was given a nearly identical target (Illustration 20). She did not quite get the B, and also had to try more than once.

Many years later, working with an independent group interested in developing this type of psychic feat, I was given an ABC target (Illustration 21) in a sealed envelope. I had no expectation that it contained letters. I recall it was a difficult target, but when I recognized the A, I concluded that the target must represent letters. You will note that I did not get them all.

But it was a beginning.

It is, of course, very exhilarating to achieve the spontaneous high-stage successes these illustrations represent, and results like these do identify the potential superpsychic. But to learn from them, you need examples of core ESP when it is *malfunctioning*. It is the malfunctioning that makes it possible to find out what to fix or control. Without lots of these malfunctioning examples, little growth is possible.

Later in this book we will look at the similarities among malfunctioning ESP results, and learn to identify the malfunctioning ESP attribute. Taken as a whole, the subjects did not "get" the target material except through layers of "noise." What will be important about studying these "noisy results" is that in all the cases the noise or the malfunctions are identical in all the individuals who attempted numerous ESP tests.

This shows that we all have identical mental levels through which the incoming ESP information can be processed, or "misprocessed." When you try your own experiments, it will be the partial results that will teach you the most about your own core ESP.

△ **TEN** △

The Influence of Disbelief and Trusting the Deeper Self

As you go about trying to locate your own ESP core potentials, you should understand, in advance, that what you *believe* about the existence of psychic talents can play a part in your ultimate success.

If an individual's ESP mind mound has a bunch of rubbish and ideas on it that tell him extrasensory perception and external sensing do not exist, then that individual might have difficulty in experiencing the nature of his own psychic nucleus. He has a psychic nucleus whether he likes the idea or not, but the acquired learning of his consciousness can suppress any hint of it.

Imagine the following scene. A disbeliever's ESP core tries to send upward into consciousness a bit of second-reality information that may be beneficial to the disbeliever. His consciousness and its acquired patterns can't tolerate this and hastily marshal a group of bits from consciousness that rush downward to obliterate the incoming psychic information. It's much like the white cells in the bloodstream rushing to collect around and destroy a foreign virus or bacterium. The white blood cells are part of a natural defense system. If it is true that all humans possess a psychic nucleus and an ESP core, then the conscious defense system against incoming psychic information is, to some degree, unnatural, sort of a culturally induced immunization against psychic experience.

Disbelief has certain powers over an individual's thought processes and over how he responds to events in the world around him. A person who disbelieves something seldom sees facts attesting to the inaccuracy of the disbelief. The old adage that people see only what they want to see is frequently true, and especially regarding psychic talents—even their *own* psychic talents.

Many of the greatest detractors of psychical research are those individuals who have admitted that if psychic talents truly exist, then their entire world view will be proved wrong. What they are referring to, of course, is not reality as it remains to be discovered by advancing science. New realities are being uncovered all the time. They are referring to a balance of their individual reality, a mental balance made up of acquired experience and learning (or mislearning).

Unless these critics can prove that they know everything that is to be known, they are out of order in rejecting the realities of ESP and its related phenomena. The evidence substantiating their reality is just too abundant and too profound. Nonetheless, the critics' realities *are* their realities, and for them, ESP truly does not exist. This *is* a reality. It involves only the disbeliever, not the psychic nuclei of all other humans. And that *is* another reality.

If you think about it, there can be no such thing as opposing realities. What is real is, simply, real. If people think two realities oppose each other, then there is something wrong with one or both those "realities."

There is no evidence for "opposing realities" in the natural universe or the cosmos. In fact, the natural universe and the cosmos exhibit a highly refined harmony of realities, the nature of which has only recently begun to astonish cosmologists. Some of the components of this harmony might seem cruel, such as all life forms having to devour other life forms (lions eating gazelles, for example) in order to survive. But behind those apparent cruelties lie the greater harmonies of the ecosystem.

Man appears to be the only life form that artificially creates realities, and these pseudorealities often do oppose each other. Frequently they are constructed so that they exclude many things that are actually real.

If an individual's mind is strongly structured against the existence of ESP, it is easy to assume he will not like to see it emerge in himself—or in others. An individual who is benignly disposed toward the existence of ESP will stand a better chance of it emerging when he attempts a psychic test. This has proved to be the case under rigorous research in which both believers and disbelievers in ESP have been tested.

Dr. Gertrude Schmeidler, one of America's leading parapsychologists, is also an insightful person who can identify closely with the human problems of ESP. She has, during her long career, conducted many unprejudiced experiments about the basic nature of psychic talents and authored many seminal papers and books on the subject.

As early as 1945, Dr. Schmeidler took an interest in the question of how believers and disbelievers would score on ESP tests. She labeled the believers "sheep" and the disbelievers "goats." She published her first paper, "Separating the Sheep from the Goats," in 1945, in the *Journal of the American Society for Psychical Research*. As a result, the sheep-goats hypothesis came into vogue as a general concept in parapsychology relating to the effect of belief and attitude to success in ESP scoring.

Dr. Schmeidler conducted lengthy, well-controlled experiments, by first dividing her subjects into two groups. The averaging of the ESP scores demonstrated that the sheep scored better than the goats did. The average scoring differences were small, but Dr. Schmeidler's data base was large enough to make the difference statistically significant.

Some of the individual sheep actually scored relatively high, while many of the goats scored quite low. Later similar experiments by others confirmed these findings, and the hypothesis that believers in ESP generally fare better in designed ESP tests has now become commonplace in parapsychology. I think we can concede that disbelief, if it is truly strong, can have a devastating effect over the natural and spontaneous workings of one's own psychic nucleus and ESP core.

We should also bear in mind that, from available statistics, the true disbeliever is in the distinct minority. Approximately 80 percent or better of the population believe in the existence of ESP, and even in academia—normally strongly structured against ESP—samples show that probably as much as 60 percent accept the probability of ESP, and another 20 percent are waiting for it to be proved.

Thus, activation of the ESP core might be simple for some, harder for others, and perhaps virtually impossible for the few that have acquired a cultural immunization against ESP and the workings of their own psychic nucleus.

Trusting the Deeper Self

Most of us have a good ideal of familiarity with our minds, even though we may not know or understand the latest psychological labels for its different parts. If we are honest, these parts are frequently an unruly lot. Few and far between are those individuals who can bring discipline into the whole show. What usually happens is that we bring discipline into those areas of our minds that are important to us, sometimes only after experience has demonstrated the painful desirability for doing so.

Getting along with one's peers and "making it" in life require mental self-discipline in several areas. Mental self-discipline is the factor that brings one into phase (into coherence) with whatever one wishes to take part in and succeed in doing.

The upward creative life is actually a series of cooperations, as any self-achiever understands, but self-discipline is the prerequisite for any cooperation. Conversely, the downward destructive life has its basis in a lack of self-discipline, the result of which is that the individual is always at odds not only with himself, but with life around him.

There are probably many types of self-discipline; but for the purpose of this book, four seem to be important. Discipline is a product of training, of focusing, of experience, and of intuition. The first three can be derived from learning and education and concern those areas where a lot of information is available to us. We can model ourselves after the elements of that information and discipline ourselves by doing so.

In areas where not much information is available to us, we have to resort to intuition alone. At the present time, the state of the art concerning extrasensory perception provides little in the way of dependable information about it. Any developed psychic that emerges in our present culture has learned to cooperate with his or her psychic nucleus and the raw core ESP processes that emerge from it. But this learning, and the self-disciplines that accompany it, is more intuitive than anything else.

There is a model that can help make this more clear. I've used the analogy of the mind mound. We all possess several different kinds of mind mounds, as, for example, one we might call the creativity mind mound. At its center is the creativity core, or the creativity nucleus.

Like the psychic nucleus, the creativity nucleus is probably part of the deeper self.

Any achieved creator—whether artist, inventor, ecologist, or businessperson—has intuitively learned to cut through the rubbish and contact the core. The creativity core seems to work on its own and works best without too much deliberate intervention by our patterns of consciousness. The achieved creator has learned, intuitively, to accommodate the elements and needs of the creativity core, and to discipline the elements of consciousness that might tend to interfere with it.

High-stage creativity is almost always as spontaneous as high-stage ESP. What the artist or inventor has learned to do is to allow the core to function without imposing rational consciousness upon it to any detrimental degree.

This situation has been expressed in different ways by many highly achieved individuals. The noted physicist, Louis de Broglie, remarked that intuition enables us to perceive all at once some profound aspect of reality by a kind of inner light that has nothing to do with laborious deductive schemes consciousness might wish to impose. The French chemist, Louis Pasteur, upon his admission to the Académie des Sciences in Paris, made a speech which must have seemed audacious to his more rationalistic colleagues. Among other things, he noted:

> The more valuable notions that the human mind possesses are all in darkness, in the background. If we were cut off from this background, the exact sciences themselves would be stripped of the greatness which derives from the secret affinity between them and other truths of infinite scope that we are beginning dimly to apprehend, and which constitute a link with the mystery of creation.

When an individual allows himself to be dominated

solely by those elements that consciousness holds, that same consciousness is quite likely to filter out impressions, information, and perceptions coming in from places other than through his frontal consciousness.

This problem can be quite severe. Psychotherapists are very familiar with how difficult it is to get the unconscious to disgorge some content that consciousness has repressed in the first place. In those cases in which creativity and ESP are being suppressed, the individual has little chance of penetrating the cores and instituting the mental disciplines necessary for their fulfillment.

Most of us live without much direct communion with our deeper self, which is therefore relegated into a condition of trying to shove bits and pieces of information upward into consciousness. Consciousness then deals with these bits and pieces in ways characteristic of the individual.

The individual who intuitively learns to accommodate the larger deeper self—and to self-discipline consciousness accordingly—is a receiver of information. In fact, the deeper self can completely resolve issues that consciousness is involved with but cannot resolve on its own. The amount of evidence for this is huge. Musicians have seen completed scores, inventors completed inventions, artists completed paintings or sculptures, mathematicians completed formulae, and so forth, all in the flick of a moment during which conscious involvement attenuated and allowed the deeper self to shove upward the completed problem.

The same is true for spontaneous high-stage ESP. There are thousands of reports where individuals have received complete information about distant events with a clarity that is visual, sensual, and intellectual all at once. The normal barriers against this kind of intrusion go down temporarily. As some have put it, the normal meshes in the net of consciousness are capable of enlargement, and widen upon these occasions.

Whatever the case may be, the problem is not so much *developing* one's extrasensory perceptions, as learning how to *prevent* interference with them.

The developed psychic has learned to do this intuitively; to switch gears, so to speak, to shift focus from consciousness to a communion with his or her deeper self and the elements of the psychic nucleus and its ESP core. In other words, the developed psychic creates an unimpeded pathway from the deeper self to conscious awareness in which the incoming psychic information can be perceived with relative clarity.

In psychic parlance, this is often referred to as "focusing." But focusing is only one half of the picture. Focusing should mean to bring into alignment the elements of consciousness that are necessary to create the pathway (or aperture) through which the psychic information travels upward to conscious perception.

The other half of the situation involves establishing a communion between the deeper self and the self as a whole. If what advanced physicists and thinkers are hypothesizing is true, that the deeper self is *already* interconnected to universal information (as discussed earlier in this book), then the deeper self doesn't need to be developed or focused. It needs only to be afforded the opportunity to deliver.

The developed psychic has learned to intuitively trust the deeper self, and has self-disciplined the avenues in the mind that can convey the information upward into consciousness.

I think we can say, with some insight now, that it takes a modicum of ESP to enlarge one's extrasensory potentials. After all, intuition is itself a variety of ESP. Locating the barriers to ESP seems to require ESP itself. Aside from this, we can see that ESP does not go on in consciousness. It is not a product of consciousness, and in fact, undisciplined patterns in consciousness only interfere with it.

Extrasensory perception's environment lies in those areas beneath consciousness where psychic information is pre-processed and emerges in a completed form.

When focusing and communion are in order, an ESP target can emerge into consciousness in a relatively un-hampered form, as we have seen via the picture drawings. Anyone interested in contacting their ESP core now has to turn his or her attention to the preconscious processes and those elements of consciousness that are likely to degrade correct transmission of the incoming psychic information.

As it turns out, picture drawings are an excellent way of doing this. Picture drawings themselves reveal what has happened to psychic information as it passes upward into consciousness. One of the good things we can say about consciousness is that it can learn, provided it can be made to understand exactly what it is supposed to *learn*. Your own picture drawings will show the way.

△ **ELEVEN** △

Taking the Plunge into Core ESP

An eagle does not make up its mind to fly: it plunges into the void and finds itself flying.

Setting Up Your Own Experiments

In setting up your own experiments, my first word of advice is to keep it simple. The simpler the experiment, the easier it will be to achieve a meaningful result.

In parapsychology, many experiments have become so complex that they probably serve to inhibit good results. In my own experience I've found that people try to overcomplicate things they don't understand very well in the first place.

The experiment and the steps you will go through should be well in your mind before you start. I've found that the ESP core processes function better when they know what will be expected of them. The typical steps are as follows:

Materials You Will Need

You will need some standard white paper. Be sure it is unlined paper, having nothing on it that will distract your attention or activate some unpredictable mental artistic activity. If the paper has lines on it, the lines tend to "drive" the spontaneous drawing into making lines. Colored paper can also help distort an accurate response. You will need a quiet atmosphere. Take the phone off the hook and turn off the radio or stereo. Use a flat table with a good light. Sit up straight in a comfortable chair. Use a sharp pencil or a narrow-tipped pen.

Selecting a Friend to Work With

Selecting the friend to work with is probably of some importance. Try to find one who is genuinely interested in the experiment, and who is not antagonistic to the idea of ESP. At an extrasensory level, emotions and attitudes actually do communicate quite easily between two people. If the friend you select is not in harmony with you or with the experiment, this "information" might become incorporated into your result and degrade it a little. Don't try working with someone who teases you or kibitzes. It's best to have someone who will trade off with you, letting you select objects for him while he tries to activate his own ESP core.

Types of Objects That Should Be Used

At first, these objects should be those that are easy to recognize. Bear in mind that the less information your ESP core has to process, the easier the task will be. To our eyes, all objects are more or less familiar and easy to recognize. But the ESP core processes bits and pieces of information, and the more of these there are about the target, the more difficult the effort will be. If you use a complicated target right at first, you will probably experience a confusion of bits and pieces of information.

For example, it is better to start with a single spoon rather than a whole box of silverware, a simply designed vase or jar rather than one that is elaborate with a lot of designs and pictures painted on it, a simple strand of pearls rather than a necklace that is made of lots of stones and a complicated design.

Maintaining Silence

Try to avoid any excessive talking or other bothersome little noises that might distract your attention. If you can arrange it, have a little bell your friend can ring when the object is ready. This helps eliminate any unintentional cueing that might occur through voice contact. This method is desirable in formal ESP testing but, in my opinion, not completely necessary. After all, you are not deliberately going to cheat. You will not have to.

Doing the Experiment

The basic picture drawing experiment is simplicity itself. When you feel you are ready, remain alone in one room and ask your friend to place the simple object on a table in another room. If another room is not available, the object can be placed in a closed box, or simply behind a barrier that you can't see through.

Sit up at a well-lighted table with your paper in front of you. Put the date and time on your paper.

Calm yourself; don't be nervous. Maintaining calmness might not be possible for the first few experiments. We tend to anticipate, get worked up, feel we are going to fail, or feel that we are "hot" and will get the target right away. It might take a few trials to bring about a detached poise, a sort of disinterest. When you can achieve this, the core ESP processes will work their best. This calming procedure doesn't mean that you have to spend a half hour preparing yourself, trying to put yourself into a semitrance. Try to treat the experiment like you would any other task that involves all your attention for a few moments.

When all is ready, let your ESP core do the work for you. Bear in mind that the ESP information is partly gut feeling, partly intuition, and partly a sort of automatic response that does not actively engage your conscious mental processes.

If you find yourself thinking about what the target might be, take a break, and start over again. When you draw something, don't start wondering what the drawing might represent because you will immediately experience a flood of possibilities.

Practically everyone will be a little self-conscious at first. Various kinds of emotions can surface as you begin to touch your ESP mind mound. A good way of causing them to dissipate is to note them down on your paper. Doing so will give you a record of how you feel as you try to activate your ESP core processes.

If you feel like putting words into your response, do so. After all, some attributes of a target cannot easily be sketched, such as textures, emotional feelings about the target, or the overall ambience of the target.

Ending Your Attempt

It has been my experience that the core ESP processes work fast. Don't be surprised if you make a quick few brief lines or a small drawing in a very short period of time. The ESP processes work this way. If you prolong your effort, trying to "do better," you will probably only be activating mental processes that will degrade the original psychic information. Knowing when to end the experiment is a matter of intuition coupled with experience. After a few experiments, you will get the feel of it.

Asking for Immediate Feedback

When you intuitively feel that your drawing has "fulfilled" itself, put your pen down and ask to see the target.

Compare the elements of your drawing with the elements of the target. After a few attempts, when your self-consciousness has calmed down, and you feel you are getting the hang of it, you will begin to note the specifics of the information through, and your whole ESP system will begin learning.

You might want to circle (with a red pen) the points or features of your picture drawing that correspond to the target or something in it. For example, if the target was a small square box, and you drew an angle or two, you would want to note that the angularity of the target was coming through. If the target was a pencil, and you drew one straight line, you would want to note that. If the target was a curved vase, and you drew a curve or a roundish thing, then you would want to note that you were in the ballpark.

If you do achieve a good representation of the target, be prepared for a flush of excitement—the ESP impact mentioned earlier in this book.

Comparing Your Drawing to Information in This Book

It will be important for you to study your drawings in the light of how they compare with the information in this book, especially the elements that contribute to errors, as discussed in Chapter 12. The ESP core processes seem to "learn" from this type of comparison and reinforcement. If you do an intellectual analysis of your attempt, you will find that your picture drawings will gradually improve, sometimes considerably so.

Pacing Your Experiments

General experience in parapsychology has shown that doing numerous experiments closely together seems only to collapse the fragile ESP core processes. It is best to do only one or two at a time, and then take a break of a day or two. Treat your experiments as you would any training experience. Go easy at first, and only gradually build up to the long, hard stuff. There is a natural urge in all of us to want to work hard and fast to develop a skill or talent. Bear in mind that talents and skills accumulate slowly, at some pace governed by our own internal mechanisms. ESP is no different. After a dozen or so experiments, you will find your own pace.

Types of Experiments

Using an object on a table in another room might get boring for you after a while. There are many variations you can enjoy, as suggested below.

But a word of caution. The whole point of doing any experiment is to *produce a picture drawing*. For far too long, ESP has been treated as a mentalist thing. That is, the subject focused on something and then used his or her conscious mind to figure out what the psychic information was. This technique put the psychic information exactly in that area that is also the source of most of the "noise" or misunderstanding ("error contributions"), i.e. consciousness.

What you are after is more contact with those areas beneath consciousness, those areas closer to the ESP core and its processes. These lie deeper in you, in areas that will be at first unfamiliar. Your own ESP core will produce the picture drawings for you, frequently without the aid or understanding of consciousness.

The ESP core and its processes *are* subtle systems. It is these you want to contact—not your conscious mental awareness. All too often I've seen people struggling to become psychic solely and only in their conscious minds. They make a conscious attempt to comprehend incoming psychic information, and more likely than not this is not much more than a guess.

Even more importantly, by not making a picture drawing, they have no chance at all to see how their ESP core and its processing systems are working. The picture drawing is much more than just a sketch of your conscious impressions. You will find that the picture drawing sort of draws itself, frequently without any decision-making characteristic or consciousness.

The incoming ESP information can get lost in the quagmires of consciousness. It gets added to, manipulated, thwarted, occluded, changed. The semiautomatic picture drawing undercuts all these complications. The picture drawing provides both a record of your experiments, and will show you which information the ESP core is coping with, and which information it is not.

As you will see, the picture drawing is a type of ESP language that deals with basic form-shape attributes of a given target. These basic form-shapes cannot be processed very well by conscious thinking or word descriptions alone, because in doing so, the basic form-shapes are translated into *another* type of presentation. It is in the translation processes that error contributions occur.

Your ESP core will not learn anything by this mental method. It will learn from its own picture drawings.

As long as you have a pad and pencil or pen with you, you can do any kind of experiment—but remember to keep your first experiments as simple as you can.

When the object-on-a-table experiment gets boring, your friend can put something in his pocket or in a box. You, yourself, can go into the street and try to "see" what is in the window of a store around a corner.

You can have a friend in a distant city work with you. Have him put something on the table in front of him. The only disadvantage to this is that you will not be able to have immediate feedback, and so you will not be able to compare your picture drawing to the actual target. But you can send your response to your friend, who can note which elements in it are correct or not.

Practically everything in the gigantic information pool of

the second reality can be expressed in picture drawing form.

I have also been part of a long-distance experiment (1500 miles) in which the task was to tell, at a prearranged time, what kind of music would be playing in a building I had never visited. Would the music be hard rock, classical, country, or African drums? I did this six days in a row, and successfully identified all six rhythms.

But what I did in each of these six experiments was to take a pen and paper and draw out the beats or tempos I felt coming in through my ESP core. Each of the four types of music is distinct from the other through their tempos and beats. The picture drawing told me which type of music was being played. If I had allowed only my conscious thought processes to analyze the incoming information, I would not have done so well—because my conscious mind was busy "hearing" all four types at once.

Further Adventures

After you become familiar enough with the picture drawing process, you can try more complicated adventures, such as prophecy. Choose a date and time in the future, and picture-draw the place you will be then. Naturally, this will have to be a place you have no plans to visit. Each of us probably doesn't know exactly where we will be on Saturday at four o'clock in the afternoon. Carry your picture drawing with you, and on that day at four o'clock take it out and compare it to where you happen to find yourself. Be honest. Do not "plan" your Saturday to coincide with your drawing.

You can also picture-draw the faces of people you don't know. Ask a friend to give you the name of a person, and then let your ESP core produce a picture drawing. Show it to your friend and ask him to point out the resemblances.

The sex of an unborn child can frequently be determined

through picture drawings. Lost items can be found as a result of a picture drawing. Use the lost item as the "target" and let the ESP core produce its picture drawing. Usually there will be enough information in the picture drawing to locate the item.

But all this is advanced work. When you begin, keep it simple. Work with table-top targets until you can cope with all the intricacies of the picture drawing processes.

Resist the Overtraining Urge

There is another important phenomenon that I think should be brought out as you get ready to do your own experiments. One of the mysteries (among so many) that parapsychologists have never been able to resolve, but have frequently observed, is the sudden cessation of ESP in an individual who had a recent string of hits. After a certain success rate has been reached, suddenly the whole ESP system seems to collapse, and the person goes through a period in which he cannot call the target at all, as if something in the ESP system were avoiding it altogether.

In parapsychology this is called "psi-missing" and it has dragged many elegantly designed experiments into oblivion. I've experienced this myself. It is associated with a certain inner fatigue and collapse of the psychic pathway, analogous to computer overload.

In parapsychology, experiments are often run in a very long series, giving the subject no resting time. When the subject is doing well, the researcher is likely to say "Boy, are you hot. Do a few more." And in doing those few more trials, the bottom drops out, sometimes forever. The same thing happens in gambling. An individual scores a few big ones and thinks, "Wow, I'm on a roll. . . ." And shortly, all the gains are gone.

In 1975, I turned my attention to this problem. It's like telling a long-distance runner that he has just run one hundred miles very well so why not try for another hundred. No one in his right mind would do that. The system expended energy successfully, but it needs to reload. Even cars need to stop for gas. Yet this is done all the time in parapsychology, under the ill-advised assumption that if ESP is working, that is just the time to drive it a little further.

I found the answer, or at least part of it, in a very unlikely place—muscle building. For a long time, muscle builders thought they needed to train considerably longer and harder to force muscles to develop. To some degree this is true, but the latest thinking on the problem is that you can overtrain the muscles. In fact, the overtraining principle is now being very closely adhered to in many different sports.

Muscle writer Joe Meeko, in an article entitled "Overrule the Overtraining Urge" in *Muscular Development*, October 1985, pins this down when he asks if you have ever wanted a body part to grow bigger and more defined so desperately that you constantly trained it to the limit . . . only to find it getting smaller and less impressive? This constitutes overtraining, and the rule now is that when a muscle seemingly goes "flat" and no longer feels pumped, you should stop there. Doing more is overtraining the muscle.

I've applied this principle to ESP, and to very good advantage. It seems we should not treat the development of our mental talents much differently than we are now learning to treat our physical talents. Have you ever burned the midnight oil, trying to make up for lost time in study, only to find that you can't remember anything the next day? Much the same thing appears to be true for ESP.

Our emerging ESP is a very fragile thing. Its early testing might be spontaneously successful. I call this the first-time effect. It needs to be tutored and paced, like any other talent.

The time to stop trying is when you feel your ESP is no

longer pumped up, but seems to have gone flat. Let your ESP system consolidate its gains and recover its energies. For nearly nine years, I've made it a principle to stop ESP experiments or drills or work just past that moment when I was doing excellently, and not even wait for the flat feeling to come in. The psi-missing syndrome can be avoided this way. If I keep driving myself past this point, soon the system collapses.

You should watch this carefully in your own experiments. If you succeed, stop there, rest for a while (a whole day is advisable), and proceed the next day. You will find your accuracy and endurance increases a little each time. Let your internal intuition set the pace for you, not your conscious excitement that says "Do more, more now, you are hot."

△ **TWELVE** △

Learning from Your Picture Drawings

The worst that can happen to you is that none of the elements in your picture drawing will correspond to the target object. By the usual standards that govern parapsychological expectation, this will be taken as evidence that no ESP was present. This may or may not be true. Something else may have happened.

We have to bear in mind that the pathway the psychic information has to take from the deeper self to consciousness is actually quite a long one. If the psychic information cannot get through this pathway, consciousness frequently just replaces it with some immediate impression of its own.

It is very beneficial to consider that "the information did not get through" rather than conclude that no ESP was present and that you missed the target completely. The information may have risen to some degree in those preconscious processes that cope with it, but encountered a barrier.

By telling ourselves that no ESP was present, we are

only putting one more deterrent on the ESP mind mound, which will serve to solidify the unknown barriers. It is much more emotionally encouraging to observe that the ESP pathway is still out of focus.

Basic ESP is no different than any other human talent. Few of us can execute any talent easily at first. The pole vaulter cannot possibly clear the eighteen-foot mark until his entire system has learned to collaborate with the task. But he will never do it at all if he thinks that it is impossible, or that he has no pole-vaulting talent. It is only with practice that the various components of his system can come into phase with each other. The same is true for all sports, and performing arts as well.

In my opinion, one of the greatest disservices to extrasensory perception is the fact that it has never been studied and compared with *other* human talents. It has always been thought of as such an astonishing thing that its organic elements have not even been looked for. This has led to the expectation that ESP either appears full-fledged or it is not there at all.

This is patently not the case. ESP is there, even if at a low stage, a stage so low that it does not get through the pathway.

If your first attempts do not produce any recognizable ESP information, just take a deep breath and try again, or maybe wait for another day.

As you gain in practice, you will discover that the psychic information pathway is very soft, if not mellow, in feeling, and you will learn which information to trust and work with. You will also begin to get a good idea of just how spontaneous the psychic information can be.

It is not a matter of actually focusing on the target material consciously. It is more a function of just "spotting" the incoming information that is trying to get along up the pathway. Sketch it out simply, even rather quickly. Then compare your drawing to the target material. You will see that at times *some* information is beginning to get through, and you can also note what information is being left out. Observing these facets carefully is what will allow consciousness to learn.

If you are slow at getting the whole target, don't be disappointed. Have confidence in those parts of it you do get. Confidence helps to build certainty, and increasing certainty is what will clear the pathway of barriers.

Information getting is the key concept that should lie behind your own attempts. Early on, I made the mistake of thinking that I should be able actually to see the target as with my eyes. I didn't, and was therefore disappointed. What I got, however, was information. If you keep trying, eventually you will be able to see that some information is managing to get past the barriers and that the psychic pathway is starting to get itself into focus.

Aside from no information getting through, there are seven general hurdles that need to be kept in mind. I made a list of these for myself in 1973, and they are still applicable for every beginner.

1. There will be instances in which you will not get the object at all or even any part of it. Instead, you'll get other objects surrounding it. Sometimes you'll pick up the thoughts of the person who put it there for you, or something in his pockets or in her purse. This is easy enough to understand. In the second reality, there is a wide spectrum of information available, and precision might be a little flexible. If your picture drawing does not correspond to the target, have a look around for something else it might resemble.

2. Often you will not have identified the object, but will have gone on to draw something from your own experience that the object reminds you of. This constitutes a replacement of the psychic information with some information that doesn't belong to it. But the psychic information rose along the pathway to trigger a comparable image in your imagination. This type of "mistake" is actually very

common. With practice, you will soon be able to recognize, internally, when this is taking place.

3. There will be instances in which you get a lot of drawings or marks or words which do not make any sense to your consciousness. They will not "go together" properly to make a recognizable picture drawing. But when you finally see the hidden object, you will be able to recognize how totally appropriate the elements are. I've termed this kind of thing "lack of fusion." You got all the rudiments, but they did not fuse into an appropriate form. There are several good examples in the illustrations below that show the exact nature of this phenomenon. Instances of lack of fusion are actually very meaningful. You can learn many things from them about how the information pathway is behaving. Lack of fusion means that there is a good deal of information coming through about the object, but that the preconscious processes are not combining it into its proper form. Lack of fusion frequently happens when the target is too complex. It tends to disappear after the ESP core becomes capable of handling complex information.

4. Sometimes in your drawing or your writing (if there is any), you may have sketched the object quite well, but have called it something other than what it is. This happens when the conscious processes do not recognize the sketch, but are determined to call it something anyway.

5. There will be other instances in which only portions are perceived, such as the details but not the major object; or conversely, the general outline of the object, but not the details.

6. Often you will get only one part of the object while the remainder of it is not perceived.

7. Other times you will get a good correspondence to the object, but there will be some distortion.

When none of these hurdles is blocking the pathway, many of you will experience instances of indisputable correspondence between your impressions and whatever the concealed object is.

In 1975, after I had the opportunity to study examples of core ESP picture drawings, I made a list of their common characteristics. This list is certainly not complete, and many of you will be able to add to it. It may be helpful to use it, and the examples provided, to compare to your early results.

Take the list and collate it with your own results. Label each element in your result accordingly. Don't just mentally compare, but actually write out next to each element the type of phenomenon it represents. This allows your conscious system to learn. As your core learns to cope with each of the many manifestations of its raw talent, you will see patterns emerge.

I've been able to identify four general categories into which all picture drawings can be grouped. I've termed these according to their importance in the ESP learning process.

ERROR CONTRIBUTIONS

ASSOCIATIONS

LACK OF FUSION

ACCURACIES

Error Contributions

Contrary to the usual approach, which concentrates only on accuracy, error contributions are actually more important to the learning process. Error contributions are *barriers* in the ESP pathway that must be identified. We learn best from our mistakes. But if we can't locate them, they cannot serve us. If you want to learn to do something well, you have to know the areas in which you are doing it badly. You correct toward greater accuracy and performance by locating and resolving or disciplining the areas of error (debugging the system).

There are four major error contributions along the ESP pathway. These probably exist near frontal consciousness, or in the areas just beneath it.

1. Some other thoughts that have nothing to do with the target or experiment
2. No contact or correspondence at all (barriers)
3. Illusion or imagination
4. False guesses, or just guessing

It is of some importance to learn to discern these features when they take place. Have the courage to admit you are just guessing if you find that you are. The system learns from self-admission. All these error contributions are barriers to the incoming ESP information. They probably show that consciousness is trying to dominate the psychic pathway.

A few examples of error contributions follow.

Illustration 22

TARGET   RESPONSE

Illustration 22, done by the young Graf S. in 1888, with the exception of the verticalness of the numeral 1, in his response Graf obviously was a victim of his imagination. The response has little to do with the target, so we can assume the cup-like response was a mind manifestation contributed by some other part of the mental processes trying to identify the target. Much the same is true of the following example. Graf got the circle part of the target, but then his imagination elaborated upon it, turning it into a comet.

Illustration 23

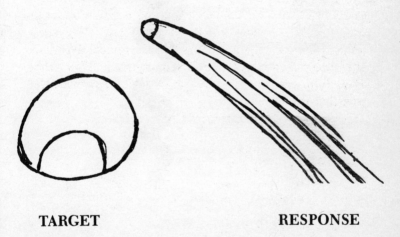

TARGET   RESPONSE

But even so, neither of these two targets and their responses are totally wrong. The actual shapes of the targets were incorporated into the responses. These two examples show that some basic information was getting through, but was subsequently overlaid with imaginative error contributions.

In the example below, taken from the Schmoll-Maibre experiments of 1889, we can see that at first the subject got the general concept of the target, but then went on into imagination. The basically correct form was changed three times, ending up with only the top part of the target. All the basic elements of the target are in the four responses, but equally evident is the work of imagination trying to "make sense" of the incoming psychic information.

Illustration 24

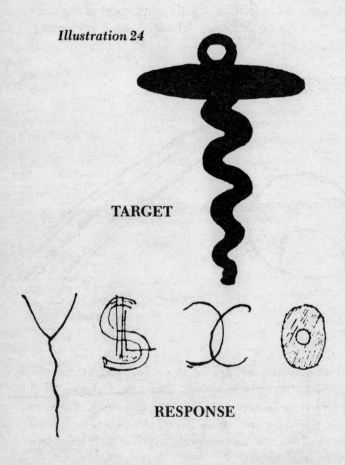

TARGET

RESPONSE

Frequently, right at the outset of an experiment, the subject gets the target correctly. But there seems to be a mental function in the whole ESP process that "doubts."

Illustration 25

TARGET

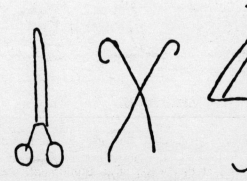

RESPONSE

It takes a perfectly valid response and converts it into one that is purely imagery. In Illustration 25 (Schmoll-Maibre, 1889), the scissors were converted into an umbrella.

In the following example (Warcollier, 1925), the target funnel was converted into an elaborate dish-vase with antler-like handles. The only correct attribute is the "containerness" showing that the correct basic information had entered the ESP core but was then altered by imagination.

Illustration 26

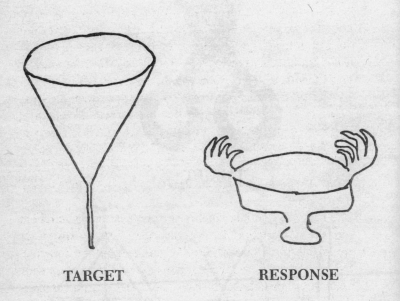

TARGET   RESPONSE

These imaginative error contributions can be found throughout the history of all picture drawings. In the 1970s at SRI International, an anonymous subject, an official who claimed he had no ESP, produced the following two examples of imaginative overlay. In these cases, the targets were not drawings, but objects in another room.

In the first example, the target was a tripod stand. The subject's response shows that the tripod feature was correctly perceived in the ESP system, but that the imagination of the man went to work and contributed the tea pot, the tray, and so forth. Normally, this kind of response would be considered a "miss." But actually it is not. What the response actually shows is some correct information in the ESP pathway *and* imaginative error contributions. The tripod concept is really quite unique, and it was this uniqueness that had entered the ESP core.

In the second example, from the same subject, the target was a food mill (which is also an example of a too complex target for beginners). In his first attempt, the subject actually got the correct shape-form, but immediately his imagination took over, calling it first an andiron and then building it up imaginatively into a bellows.

While each of these error contribution examples provided undesirable results in the strict sense of accuracy, each of them illustrated two things: Some basic information was included in the responses, and with careful attention to the responses, the individual can learn how imagination is seeking to resolve the mysterious ESP information.

When you evaluate your own picture drawings, circle in red the information in the response that is correct or applicable to the target, and in green, label the imaginative overlays. The entire ESP core system learns this way. Soon your responses will have more red-circled information in them than green notes signifying imagination. As your red begins to predominate, you will gain in confidence.

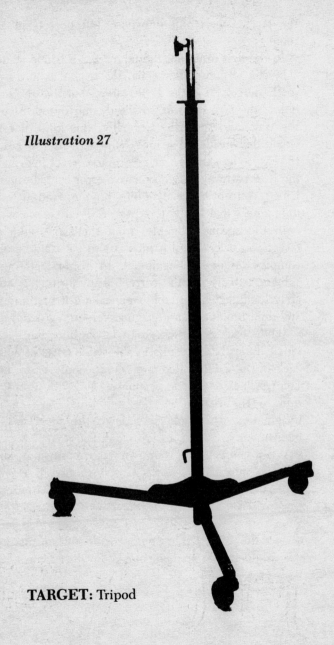

Illustration 27

TARGET: Tripod

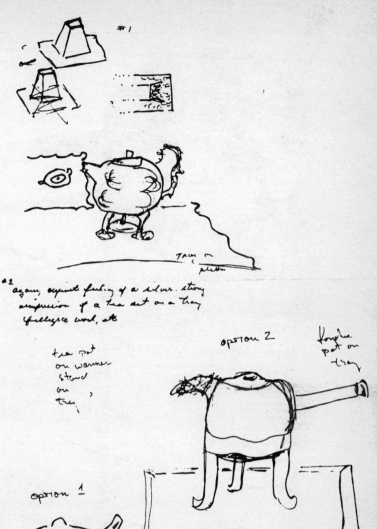

#1

#2 "again, against feeling of a silver. strong
suspicion of a tea set on a tray
(ellipse word, etc

tea pot
on warmer
stand
on
tray ?

option 2

tongue
pot on
tray
?

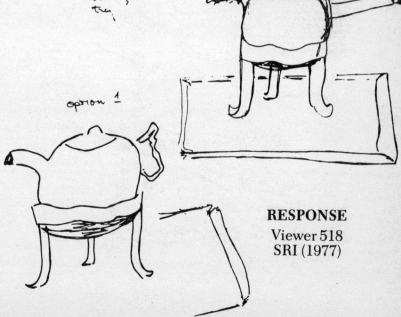

option 1

RESPONSE
Viewer 518
SRI (1977)

Illustration 28

TARGET: Food Mill

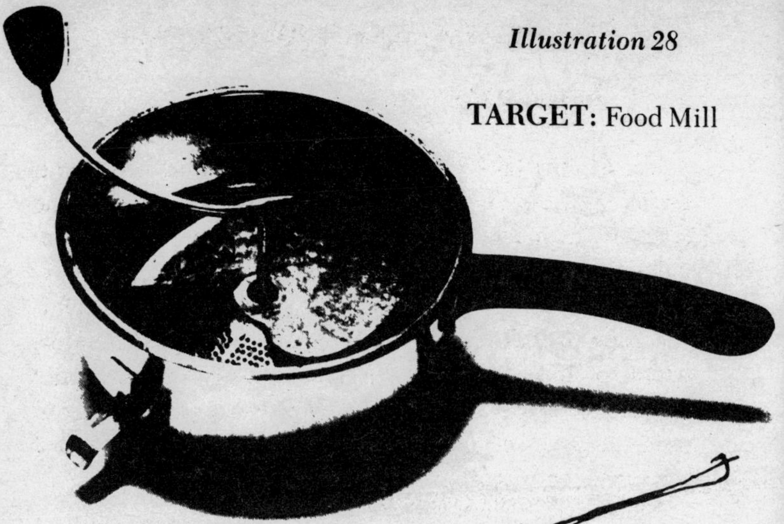

RESPONSE
Viewer 518
SRI (1977)

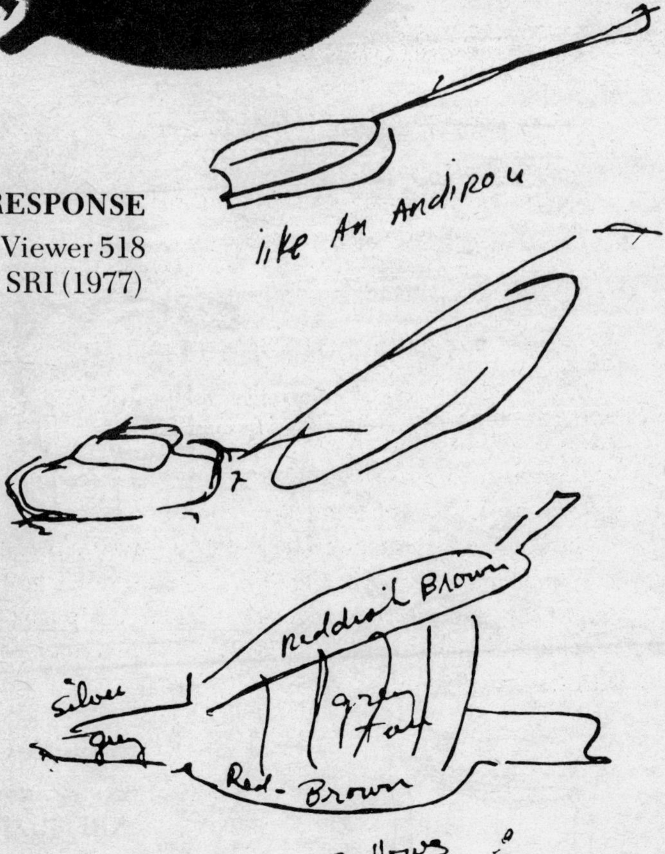

like An Andiroน

reddish Brown

Silver
gray

gray
Flat

Red - Brown

Bellows

Associations

Associations take place when the incoming ESP information gets far enough into the system to trigger some sympathetic image, feeling, taste, or smell, etc., but not far enough to objectively emerge as a totally correct drawing. These sympathetic responses are quite common. Referring back to the example of Napoleon, the psychic information of Josephine's death penetrated far enough into Napoleon's own ESP system to trigger fears and grief, but not far enough into his consciousness to deliver the actual or accurate information.

I've identified four major types of associations:

1. Not the object itself, but things associated with it or, in some cases, things that might be expected in association with it
2. Associations of feelings, etc.
3. Something the object (or location) reminds you of
4. An image of something similar to the object

In the example below (Miss Relph, 1883), the target was a sketch of a line looped into circles. Miss Relph said "she seemed to see a lot of rings, as if they were moving, and she could not get them steadily before her eyes."

The correct information had entered Miss Relph's ESP core but had stimulated a feeling (association) of motion, which she gave as her primary response. Her picture drawing was an estimation of the form of the target mixed with her association.

Illustration 29

TARGET

RESPONSE

In the following example (Schmoll-Maibre, 1898), the associations have triggered imagination, resulting in three very elaborate responses. The concept of "arrowness" had definitely entered the ESP core. The first response is, in fact, quite correct, but the system seemed to want to incorporate the association of speed or motion into the picture drawing. Seen in this light, two of the responses are absolutely correct, while the middle one is less so.

Illustration 30

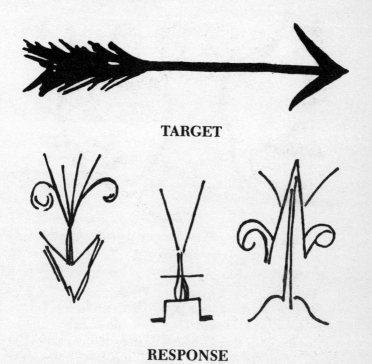

TARGET

RESPONSE

In the following example (Schmoll-Maibre, 1898), the cat information had obviously entered the ESP core of the subject, but was quickly (and accurately) converted into a cat association. The response shows not the cat of the target, but an association in the subject's ESP pathway. This example is a very good one showing the conversion of an actual target into a general idea, several examples of which we have seen earlier in this book.

Illustration 31

TARGET   **RESPONSE**

In the following example (Warcollier, 1948), the target was a sketch of a hanged man with, presumably, some crows or buzzards flying about—a rather grim target. The subject's response was a mixture of associations of something swinging and flying. The response is at some distance from the actual forms of the target, showing that the target might have been too complex and that the mind manifestations focused only on an all-inclusive association of the target's major elements. Even so, the response is not totally wrong.

Illustration 32

TARGET   **RESPONSE**

In the next example (Warcollier, 1948), the angular shapes, in the subject's mind-manifesting processes, clearly associated to a banner. The target is, simply, too complex to start with. Even when viewed by the eye, it might not be recognized as anything. But the association mechanisms in the ESP pathway converted it into something that is not completely incorrect. Association "solved" the incoming information by merging all the angles into one discrete image.

Illustration 33

TARGET   RESPONSE

Obviously, associations of this type are not desirable since they do turn targets into something they are not. But it is only by gentle learning that the ESP core and the pathway will eventually learn that it doesn't need to "solve" all incoming information in this manner. Take your pen and label the associations as such. Eventually, they will decline when the whole ESP core realizes that it doesn't need to contribute through "solutions" of this kind.

The next example (Warcollier, 1925) is truly interesting. In 1924, the members of his New York group were trying to transmit to the Paris group. The target selected for this long-distance experiment was the idea of a cobra, coiled and hissing, ready to strike. In Paris, at the appointed hour, Warcollier got the idea of the "movement of the reptile," and illustrated his impression as follows.

Illustration 34

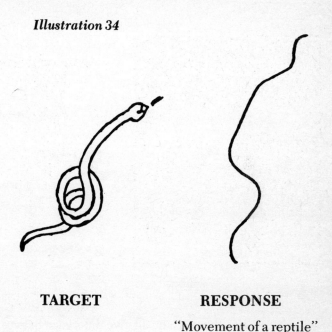

TARGET   **RESPONSE**

"Movement of a reptile"

Like Miss Relph's motion response illustrated on page 150, Warcollier's response is exact—but it is an association since the target was a sketch and had no literal motion in it.

In another experiment, this time from room to room in Paris, the target was a sketch of a giraffe's neck and head. In this case the association was a *word*. The general idea of a giraffe had been processed so far upward that it could correctly be turned over to wording. Then Warcollier (the subject) drew four "ice cream cone–like" things, which can loosely be interpreted as the animal's ears and horns. But the totality of the response is an associative one—not a rendering of the target itself.

Illustration 35

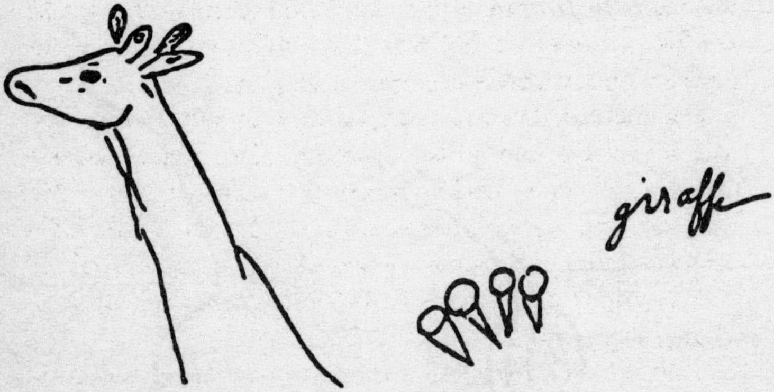

TARGET   RESPONSE

As you can see, there is a qualitative difference between pure error contributions by imagination and associative contributions. The former seeks to falsely solve the ESP information through imagination, but the latter is trying to incorporate the ESP information into a legitimate referencing framework—and often succeeds remarkably well. But the actual form-shape of the target remains in that part of the ESP pathway that is still beneath consciousness.

In doing your own experiments, label your relevant associations in red—they are, after all, correct information, although processed through associations. Associations tend to decrease as confidence in basic ESP rises. Meanwhile, by identifying and labeling them, the whole system will learn.

Lack of Fusion

Lack of fusion is one of the more important concepts that needs to be understood. In terms of the ESP core and the pathway, it means that the components of the target are being perceived but that they "won't go together" to form an understandable image or concept.

The picture drawing emerges as bits and pieces, but will not evolve into a distinct image. The subject usually experiences some kind of stress or confusion when this happens, and can become so irritated that the whole ESP core collapses as a result. Normally, we would think of this as definitely destructive. But not if you really look at what is happening.

Lack of fusion frequently occurs *without* imagination or associations poking into the response. The incoming psychic information is not being diverted into these "helpful" channels. In fact, lack of fusion shows that the ESP core is trying to cope with the information on its own—without assistance.

Thus, when lack of fusion emerges in the picture drawings, it is a hopeful and positive signal that the ESP core has been activated, and that the whole system pathway is retreating from trying automatic resolutions to the information. When lack of fusion does occur then, it is an indication that soon the activated ESP core will "learn" to cope on its own with shape-form, etc. Conscious extrapolation has retreated or ceased, and so false imaginings soon go away.

So, far from being the mess it at first appears to be, lack of fusion is characteristic of the ESP core's learning.

Some types of lack of fusion are shown in the examples below. Some of these examples are rather blatant, but others are somewhat subtle. Study them—and your own efforts—with some attention. It is too bad that lack of fusion has not been understood before now for what it truly represents. It represents a pattern of learning and growth; not the deleterious phenomenon it was thought of in the past.

Lack of fusion occurs when the whole system has learned from imagination and from associations. These do stop or at least decline. But at the same time, the developing psychic pathway is yet too weak to deal with information which is actually coming through in bits and pieces. It might also be a sign that the target selected by your friend is actually too complex. Just ask him to select simpler targets.

There are at least four variations on lack of fusion, but they differ only in degree.

1. All parts are correctly perceived, but will not connect to form a whole.
2. Some parts are fused; others are not.
3. Fusion is only approximate.
4. Parts are incorrectly fused; all parts are there, but put together in such a way as to falsely create another image.

An example from Sinclair (1930) illustrates lack of fusion so well that it alone might suffice to serve as representative of all. The target was a swastika, and the subject, Mary Craig Sinclair, labored over her impressions to a point where she finally gave up and said, "These will not go together."

Illustration 36

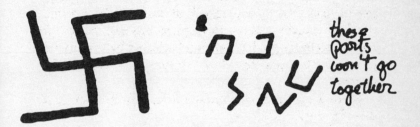

TARGET   **RESPONSE**

In another instance where the target was a sketch of two boxing stick figures, Mrs. Sinclair had an equally hard time of it.

Illustration 37

TARGET   **RESPONSE**

Almost exactly like Mrs. Sinclair's problems with the swastika, Warcollier reports an experiment using a target divided by a large cross into four parts. This target is similar in many ways to the swastika target, but even more important, the lack of fusion responses are nearly identical also, as shown below.

Illustration 38

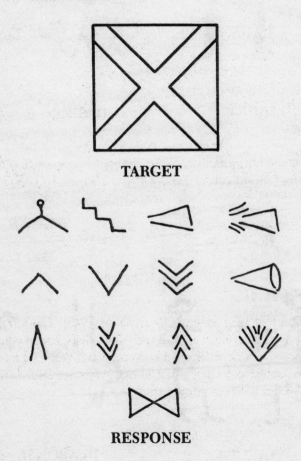

TARGET

RESPONSE

Lack of fusion is often first apparent when the target is too complex for the individual's ESP core. The targets seem easy enough for our eye, but in fact are quite complex for the inexperienced ESP core.

Another classic case of lack of fusion (Schrenck-Notzing, 1890) was Frau E.'s attempt to get a target composed of a badly sketched six-pointed star. After five attempts she apparently gave up.

Illustration 39

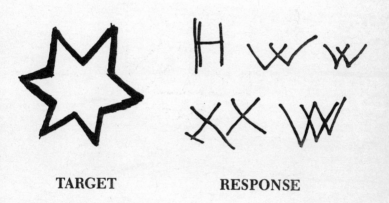

TARGET   RESPONSE

The following example (Warcollier, 1948) shows an impressive gathering of appropriate information, but an equally impressive lack of fusion. The target was a sketched blimp. The subject got a large part of the important information, but it did not fuse into its whole.

Illustration 40

TARGET

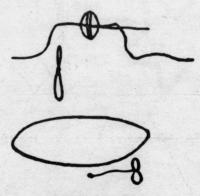

RESPONSE

While George Albert Smith, in 1883, was the first to produce high-quality picture drawings, he, too, experienced lack-of-fusion problems. In the following example, the target was composed of an oval on top of a triangle, both with a cross in them. Smith reported, "I can see a three-cornered thing, and there's a thing like a duck's egg somewhere." He also mentioned that he had an impression of a cross right over the egg.

Illustration 41

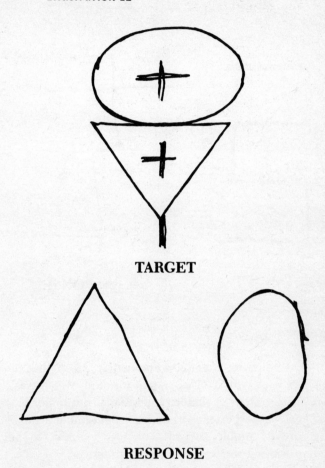

TARGET

RESPONSE

In the above example, while Smith got the two most important elements of the target, they would not fuse into the correct relationship. Some information is missing, although Smith felt there was a cross somewhere.

Another example from Smith, below, shows approximate fusion, although the general idea is there also.

Illustration 42

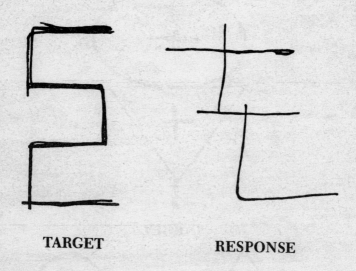

TARGET   RESPONSE

In the following example, Fraulein A. (1898) had fusion problems with a black square inside of which was a white circle. To us, a simple target really. But to her ESP core and its inexperienced pathway, this simple arrangement proved problematic. It only partly fused, as her picture drawing shows, on the third attempt.

TARGET Ultramodern Dome House

Illustration 43

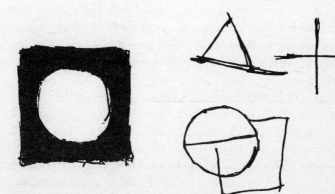

TARGET   **RESPONSE**

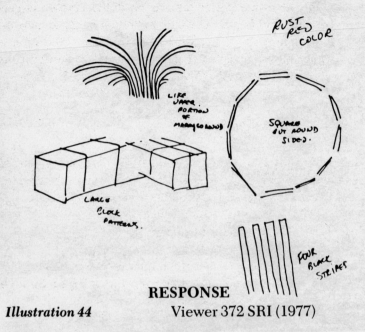

RESPONSE

Illustration 44   Viewer 372 SRI (1977)

In the above example (SRI International, 1979), the target was a free-form home some distance from the experiment room. The subject first (correctly) perceived the target as a series of large blocks; but then when the curving nature began to be processed, he experienced lack of fusion. The four black stripes at the bottom of the response may refer to the black wrought iron fence at the site.

Lack of fusion comes and goes during experiments. As mentioned, its presence is a good indicator that the ESP core is about to become more efficient. It is also a signal that perhaps the target is too difficult for the ESP core's present capabilities, and once in a while, it is an indication of fatigue—in the ESP core itself, not physical or mental fatigue. If the latter are present, one should not attempt an experiment in the first place. Core fatigue simply means that you are overtraining.

In your own experiments, start with the simplest targets possible, and as you continue, only then begin to increase their complexity. This will take some time, but after a while you will be able to compare your most recent results with those you achieved when you first started.

Accuracies

There can be many different types of accuracy, out of which I've listed eleven of the most commonly encountered:

1. Correct, in all aspects
2. Correct, but some distortion
3. Correct, but something else added
4. Correct, but some information missing
5. Correct, but information developed through two or more attempts
6. Only part or parts perceived
7. Details perceived, but not the whole
8. Correct relationships perceived
9. General idea correct
10. Correct, but overdeveloped
11. Correct, but elements reversed

Like error contributions, accuracies should be especially studied. We learn from them, too, and they build our system's confidence, and develop trust in the peculiar rules and laws the psychic nucleus and the ESP core seem to be following.

In the following example (G. A. Smith, 1883), the response is correct but its elements are reversed; this may also represent a lack of fusion, technically so. But the head and the square are reversed, although both correct.

Illustration 45

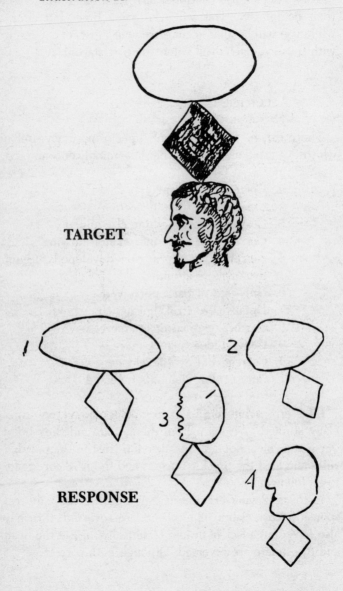

TARGET

RESPONSE

In the following example (Miss Relph, 1884), the processed information is correct, but reversed.

Illustration 46

TARGET   **RESPONSE**

An example of a correct, but overdeveloped response is shown below (Fraulein E., 1890).

Illustration 47

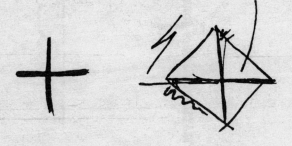

TARGET   **RESPONSE**

In the example below, the general idea is correct (Miss Edwards, 1884).

Illustration 48

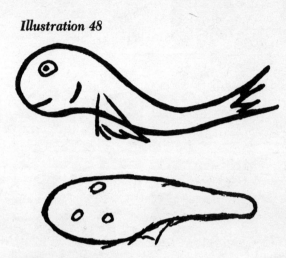

RESPONSE

TARGET
Miss E. almost directly said, "Are you thinking of the bottom of the sea, with shells and fishes?" and then, "Is it a snail or a fish?" —then drew as above.

In the following example, an SRI remote viewer saw only parts of the distant house that had been selected as a target. His ESP core processed some of the information involving the window turret and the porch pilasters, resulting in a response that was only partially correct with vast amounts of other information missing.

TARGET: Victorian House

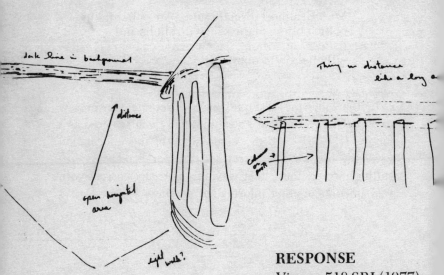

Illustration 49

RESPONSE
Viewer 518 SRI (1977)

Below is an example (Miss Edwards, 1884) showing that only part of the target information had been processed, but that part was correct.

Illustration 50

TARGET　　　　　　　　　　**RESPONSE**

The following is a superb example (Schmoll-Maibre, 1898) illustrating correct information developed through two or more attempts. Only a small portion of information is missing.

Illustration 51

TARGET

RESPONSE

In the following experiment, a watch was used for the target (Sinclair, 1930). Mrs. Sinclair drew most of the information, but there was also some missing.

Illustration 52

TARGET　　　　　　　　**RESPONSE**

In the following illustration (Warcollier, 1945), the subject processed the major part of the target's information— and then went on to add something uniquely of his own imagination. This is a good example of the basic response being correct, but something was added.

Illustration 53

TARGET

RESPONSE

The following is an example (Warcollier, 1945) of a correct impression, but with some distortion added. There is also a great deal of information missing, but this is to be expected when the target material is too complex.

Illustration 54

TARGET

RESPONSE

Correct in all aspects literally refers to those instances in which the response contains all the correct information. There may be some target information missing, but what is given *is* correct. Frequently this will be the entire target, but if the target is large or complex, equally frequently the response will contain only parts of the target. Our eye does this naturally. It looks at a target in a sequence, first one thing and then another. Our eyes never see the entire scene simultaneously. The scene is built up, usually starting with what seems the most important or prominent, and then going on to lesser details. The ESP core appears to work much the same way.

Illustration 55

TARGET

RESPONSE

Illustration 55 (Warcollier, 1945), shows a prime example of this type of accuracy. The target was a photo of a blimp in a hangar. The psychic perception first concentrated on the most prominent part of the photo, the blimp itself, and then went on to some of the details.

A Small Test

Below are six picture drawings, together with their targets. See if you can identify the characteristics of all six before you turn to the answers following them. This is good practice for you, to get the old brain going, so to speak. I'd like to give a hundred other examples, but they can't fit into a book of this size. I heartily recommend that you get the available books on the sources of the picture drawings and look through them. There you will see the different kinds of picture drawing results in plenty.

Now, to your quick test—

Illustration 56

Number One

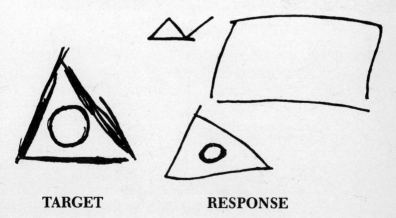

TARGET   **RESPONSE**

Illustration 57

Number Two

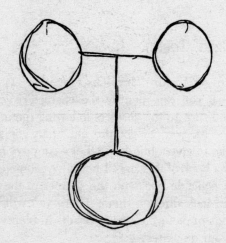

TARGET

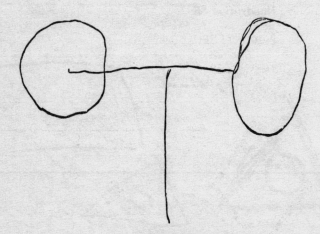

RESPONSE

Illustration 58

Number Three

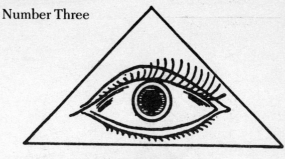

TARGET

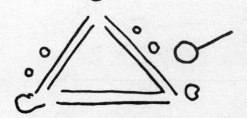

RESPONSE

Illustration 59

Number Four

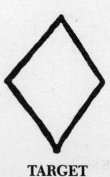

TARGET   **RESPONSE**

Illustration 60
Number Five

TARGET

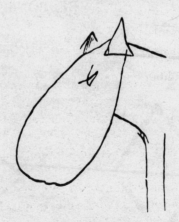

RESPONSE

Illustration 61

Number Six

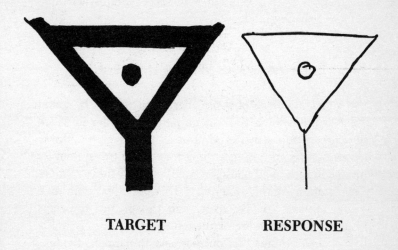

TARGET   RESPONSE

Answers

1. Correct, after two or more attempts (Fraulein E., 1890).
2. Correct, but some information missing (G. A. Smith, 1883).
3. Correct, but some information missing and some imagination added (Warcollier, 1945).
4. Lack of fusion (Sinclair, 1930).
5. General idea only (G. A. Smith, 1883).
6. Correct (Kate Smith, 1884).

As a result of this small test, you can see that it is not very difficult to grasp the different elements or qualities of a picture drawing. When you start to analyze your own, just remember that "information" is the key word. In your picture drawing, look for those elements that agree with the target. Don't say that "this must be a coincidence," as

so many parapsychologists do. We have no way of knowing if it is a coincidence or not. Assume it *is* ESP information that has gotten through the pathway. As you continue
to do picture drawings, you will soon see more and more
information getting through. The ESP core is activated
and in a learning mode.

Each Individual Will Be Different

At first, any or all of these characteristics can be found
in picture drawings. There is no particular order in which
they are to be encountered. But as the psychic pathway
becomes stronger and more integrated into the system (of
the unconscious and consciousness), a lot of these random
manifestations simply disappear. The individual's intuitive
system appears to take over, and the picture drawings
become more and more organized.

One of the things that does appear to happen, though,
is that the system grows by leaps and bounds. There may
be a first spontaneous high-stage result, followed by a
series that is plainly a mess. Suddenly, the system makes
another jump in quality, followed by yet another difficult
period. This can happen several times before the system
levels out and begins working in a predictable harmony
with the psychic nucleus.

We can assume that during these jumps and starts, the
ESP mind mound is reorganizing itself based upon actual
self-experience of the activated ESP core. So do not be
dismayed if after doing well, your experiments suddenly
appear to collapse in confusion.

THIRTEEN

The Reality Behind Picture Drawings

Psychic picture drawing began in 1882, and has resurfaced every now and then during the intervening hundred years. Taken all together, they give substance to the existence of extrasensory perception better and more completely than any other kind of evidence parapsychology has to offer.

In bringing this book to a conclusion, I'd like to point the reader's attention to what picture drawings represent in themselves, outside of being mere replicas of some given target, and the central processing difficulties individuals might experience in perceiving it.

Picture drawings have been produced by people of all different ages and from different walks and stations of life. Children and youths with no psychic experience at all can produce them as well as a mature, developed psychic.

Picture drawings you produce yourself are of a convincing nature, insofar as we can be convinced of anything. René Warcollier, in his 1945 book *Mind to Mind*, made the most explicit statement about them when he noted that he had no doubt at all that the drawing technique as a whole, using any statistically valid method of assessment, is truly repeatable, in the sense that any who care to try will obtain substantially the same results as have others. He went on to say that he believed that those who try such experiments themselves will be convinced.

But convinced of what? Warcollier was working within the telepathy concept, using senders and receivers from Paris to New York, or wherever. So it appeared to them that "telepathy" was the active force that lay behind the picture drawings themselves. But since his time, picture drawings also have been produced outside the telepathy concept; from inanimate nondescript objects, from objects hidden in cans or located halfway around the world, and from experiments designed to see if a psychic could perceive a future situation that no one had yet decided upon.

To some degree, picture drawings might reinforce our current concepts of telepathy, clairvoyance, and precognition (and postcognition), but if you look at them as a whole and not as a *product* of one of these labels; they hint at a larger, more general reality.

In this book, I've shown how picture drawings undercut the problems of verbalizing and wording. Wording is culturally acquired, and divides people into language groups. But we can see that picture drawing processes commonly used words to describe an element that is not easily reducible to a picture in the first place—a feeling, an emotion, or some other delicate nuance.

I've also pointed out one particular characteristic of all the picture drawings, the fact that they are so generally alike that if one did not know they had been produced by several different people over a century, we might think they were all done by the same person. I believe a huge mistake has been made in not realizing that picture drawings are more than just sketches. They have been thought of, rather automatically, as an individual's artistic representation of his or her impressions, using art rather than words to record the psychic impressions. This is *not* the case at all.

I am an artist, as is Hella Hammid, and a few other picture drawers have been artists also. But I can assure you that I can draw much better than what occurs in picture drawings. In fact, the larger majority of picture drawers have not been artists. Many picture drawers have introduced themselves as people who can't draw; and indeed have no previous art background.

The relative ease by which picture drawings can be produced by nonartists, together with the striking similarity of all picture drawings, suggests that the drawings are not the product of an individual's artistic processes, but are a kind of basic psychic language in themselves. A language that has gone totally unnoticed by all parapsychologists.

This psychic pictolanguage has one element in common among all picture drawers. It translates the incoming psychic information into basic forms and shapes which are then recognized by the individual's psychic system and consciousness. The picture drawing mechanism seldom goes beyond this specific task, and it is unusual to find picture drawings fleshed out into highly artistic renderings. When the drawing *is* fleshed out, we are most likely to discover that it has been done so by consciousness trying to fill in the holes and that what has been filled in is erroneous.

Pristine examples of picture drawing are all a kind of psychic imaging shorthand, truncated, brief, and to the point. With experience, picture drawings do become more precise as to details and relationships, but the shorthand quality remains the same. It is this basic shape-form characteristic that causes all picture drawings to resemble each other. It is the commonality that tells us that we are dealing with a psychic language of some kind and not an individual's artistic bent.

Shape-form recognition is basic to any form of perception, as all physiologists and psychologists have known for some time. It is the primal function around which all additional perceptual systems of the organic entity are organized. Shape-form recognition normally takes place automatically, that is to say, in those parts of us that are below consciousness. If consciousness had to deliberately analyze anew every shape and form it encountered, life would be a grueling task indeed. Shape-form recognition has become automatic and spontaneous.

It is at this same nonconscious automatic and spontaneous level that psychic picture drawings are encountered. We can put together the following scenario: The deeper self is connected into the vast reaches of the second reality, where space and time are irrelevant. In the psychic mode, the psychic nucleus selects information from that reality, and the ESP core begins to process it, and give it immediate shape and form. This immediate shape-form pops out in a pictolanguage that is universal in all its characteristics. It is only at a second stage of interpretation that language components are introduced, and then in the language of an individual.

It is important to note that psychic picture drawings are unique only in their psychic aspect. Otherwise, they have close relatives in the drawings of children, in doodles, and in the structural sketches of artists, architects, and inventors.

In 1973, when I was trying to figure out just what picture drawings were, I began a search in literature *outside* the parapsychological framework. Rudolf Arnheim's well-known book *Art and Visual Perception* was particularly significant, especially Chapter IV, entitled "Growth." Among other things, this chapter deals with "Why Do Children Draw That Way?" and it contains many examples of children's drawings that are identical to the shape-form characteristics found in psychic picture drawings. Arnheim makes the revealing statement:

From the outset I have insisted that we cannot

hope to understand the nature of visual representation if we try to derive it directly from optical projections of the physical objects that constitute our world. [Artistic] pictures and sculptures of any style possess properties that cannot be explained as mere modifications of the perceptual raw material received through the senses. . . . If we assumed that the point of departure for visual experience was the optical projections supplied by the lenses of the eyes, we would expect that the earliest attempts at imagery would cleave most closely to those projections. . . . Any deviation from that model, we would expect, would be a later development, reserved for the freedom of mature sophistication. But instead, the opposite is true. The early drawings of children show neither the predicted conformity to realistic appearance nor the expected spatial projections.*

In fact, children draw via what Arnheim calls "representational concepts," which is exactly what psychic picture drawings are when we look at them closely. Representational concepts furnish the equivalent of the visual concepts we would otherwise wish to express. But the representational concepts are being manufactured somewhere within the topography of our deeper selves, and always bear preconscious processing attributes, whether in children or mature adults.

Arnheim's chapter also discusses the value of the curved, vertical, or horizontal line, and the differentiation and fusion of the parts: that is, several of the phenomena you will run into in your own psychic picture drawings. If you are going to undertake your experiments seriously, I recommend you study Arnheim's book.

*Rudolf Arnheim, *Art and Visual Perception, A Psychology of the Creative Eye*, University of California Press, Berkeley and Los Angeles, 1955 and 1974, p. 163.

While I was working on the manuscript for this book, the ideas presented in it received some unexpected analogous support from a new book that has just come into print. It reveals the importance of drawings and the unconscious phenomena that characterize the picture drawing processes.

Drawing on the Artist Within by Betty Edwards (author of *Drawing on the Right Side of the Brain*) examines in penetrating detail the basic emotional and intuitive aspect of drawings and the commonality the drawings share. Her book is filled with examples of drawings that bear close similarities to psychic picture drawings as well as the representational-concept drawings of children. She dubs these drawings "analog drawings," and the patterns produced by them suggest the universality of certain "sentic forms" observed by neurophysiologist-musician Manfred Clynes.

But whether called analog drawings, representational concepts, or psychic picture drawings, Edwards enunciates a crowning concept:

> Complexity aside, I am going to forge ahead and assume that a nonverbal, visual language of drawing exists as a possible parallel to verbal language, even though I cannot at this point spell it out. . . . A language of drawing, of course, is not the only possible parallel language. There exist, obviously, many nonverbal languages: the language of sound (music), the language of movement (dance or sports), of abstract symbolic thought (mathematics and science), of color (painting), of film (as Orwell suggested), and the language of Nature itself—the genetic code, for example. Each of these could perhaps serve equally well . . . for making thought visible.*

*Betty Edwards, *Drawing on the Artist Within*, Simon and Schuster, New York, 1986, p. 53.

Later in her book, Edwards introduces the concept "It thinks." She is referring to that interior something, beneath or beyond our consciousness, that itself is busy constructing concepts that are later pushed up into our consciousness in a relatively completed form. But we can now comprehend that this phenomenon is clearly akin to the function provided by the psychic picture drawing. The psychic picture drawing (like representational concepts or analog drawings) is a form of language the unconscious psychic "It thinks" is using to push up into consciousness its psychic nucleus perceptions of things in the universe that are invisible to our physical senses. Edwards's book is a must. Not only will it help liberate your spontaneous drawing capabilities, but it will give you an excellent grounding in the scope of this pictolanguage.

All these phenomena are, without doubt, very important in coming to grips with the essentials of the extrasensory experience. But I think there is an importance that goes far beyond that. Since the ESP core seems to be universally shared, it is much closer to universal psychic communion than are the elements of our consciousness or frontal consciousness. The modern focus on increasing individuality has done nothing at all to ameliorate the ills of the world or to resolve the dangers which seem to increase all the time.

The trend of the new age is toward self-enlightenment and a deeper communion with the energies and forces that underlie the individual, who, often operating out of attunement with the whole, is only bringing added disaster upon all.

The present trend, which began some two hundred years ago, is all toward speed and intensified individualism. As the controversial art critic Suzi Gablik has noted:

> Modernism discouraged the individual from finding any good outside himself. Today, there is still a pervasive sense that only by divorcing

themselves from any social role can artists establish their own individual identity. Freedom and social obligation are experienced in our world as polar opposites which run at cross purposes to each other. In the life of a professional, the world does not impose any mission beyond the realization of one's professional aims. . . . It strikes me more and more that as the dangers of planetary survival escalate, the practical consequences of such an attitude are becoming increasingly apparent. Our modernist notions of freedom and autonomy . . . begin to seem a touch ingenuous.*

Gablik was, of course, speaking of modern artists. But her critique can be projected into the world at large and into ESP.

In parapsychology, ESP has been viewed as an individual talent, some special individual mental-body-mind mechanism that the professional aim of parapsychology was to discover. But what if it is not this at all? What if extrasensory perception is but a vast, not particularly individual, gigantic plane that interconnects all humanity with itself and with all existence, and that developed psychics are special only in that they are better integrated into this plane, whereas all others have individuated from it for one reason or another?

This concept reverses the standard concept in parapsychology about what ESP and related psychic talents are all about. But if this concept is adopted, many apparent enigmas immediately become resolvable. For example, it explains why disbelief affects ESP. It individuates the person from the ESP plane to such a degree that he becomes disconnected from it. It explains the source of ESP information, especially as regards people. At a basic level, we are *all* interconnected.

*Suzi Gablik, "Changing Paradigms," *New Art Examiner*, June 1985, p. 20.

The implications of this are enormous; but these implications are in keeping with advanced thinking in physics, in which this interconnectedness is frequently referred to as "field theory" or "field concept." In her incisive book *The Cosmic Web,* N. Katherine Hayles has identified the concept so clearly that I can't resist quoting it.

> Perhaps most essential to the field concept is the notion that things are *interconnected.* The most rigorous formulations of this idea are found in modern physics. In marked contrast to the atomistic Newtonism idea of reality, in which physical objects are discrete and events are capable of occurring independently of one another and the observer, a field view of reality pictures objects, events, and observer as belonging inextricably to the same field; the disposition of each, in this view, is influenced— sometimes dramatically, sometimes subtly, but in every instance—by the disposition of the others.*

There are many concrete examples of this interconnectedness. Scientists now know that flocking birds in flight do not simply follow a leader as was once thought. When the flock turns, it turns as a flock, as if the flock itself is an interconnected organism. Carroll Nash, a biologist and parapsychologist, and his colleagues at St. Joseph's University in Philadelphia, have demonstrated that the growth rate of bacteria can be affected by the mental intention of a group of people concentrating on them. Many earlier experiments testing the "efficacy of prayer" showed positive results. It has also been shown that plants generally grow better in musical environments that are

---

*N. Katherine Hayles, *The Cosmic Web: Scientific Field Models and Literary Strategies in the Twentieth Century,* Cornell University Press, Ithaca and London, 1984, pp. 9–10.

harmonious—rock music causes many plants to wilt or die.

But all examples like these have one thing in common—the fact that the whole experiment is an information exchange environment at levels beneath our conscious awareness *and* the fact that consciously held mental attitudes can feed back into the information exchange system and influence it in turn.

This is exactly analogous to ESP. In environments that have a positive outlook about ESP, it tends to emerge more spontaneously. When a strong psychic emerges, ESP tends to emerge in others in his environment. The reverse is also true. I've been in at least three parapsychology laboratories where the leading figure of the lab has stated he has never seen any ESP in his presence. Reports of their work reveal no ESP or very little of it as a result of their experiments.

What is different between the two orientations is that the underlying interconnecting levels have been cut off in the negative instances, and reinforced in the positive ones. The psychic pathways in individuals *reorient themselves* in the pro environment, and soon ESP is being experienced by the majority.

All this suggests that real communion between people takes place at the extrasensory level. Mere intellectual communication does not bring people together, but sets up individuality differences which shortly can expand into conflicts.

If this is so, then the closer one is connected to one's own ESP core and psychic nucleus, the more interconnected that person is going to be with the greater realities that lie beneath conscious individuation.

If, like the hundredth monkey, there emerged one hundred people who could contact their psychic nucleus and know it to be real through self-experimentation and self-enlightenment and illumination, then we could expect to see some major shifts, not only in the incidence of real

ESP, but in the basic communal layer that interconnects all humanity. If this were increased a hundredfold by people disposed toward world peace and the resolution of the plagues of the ecosphere and biosphere, a new age might truly have dawned.

This would amount to a gigantic reintegration of the objective world with the vital elements of the second reality.

Picture drawings, on the surface so humble, serve to help you know what a hidden object might be. But in another, more important, way, they help resurrect the psychic communion factor so obviously missing in the world at large. Thus, in my opinion, confirmation of one's own ESP through the relatively simple device of picture drawing experiments is destined to play a very important role in the new age ahead. Picture drawings, as so many have discovered, are but the first step to entering the greater psychic realities; but a very important first step they are.

So find your coworker, form your experimental groups, and get on with it. I, for one, would like to hear how you fare.

INGO SWANN
c/o Bantam Books, Inc.
666 Fifth Avenue
New York, N.Y. 10103

△ FOURTEEN △

ESP and
the Future

For the first time in history, governments are expressing more than just a passing interest in the potential applications of ESP. It is an interest related not only to intelligence gathering, but alas, to the eventual use of ESP for the control of psychological behavior. Government-sponsored psychical research projects were unheard of before the late 1960s. But during those turbulent years (at the height of the cold war), a new force in parapsychology made its presence felt.

That new force is the militant and resourceful Soviet Union, which, in the late 1960s, undertook to study all aspects of ESP, most assuredly for no other reason than to discover its potential uses. To this end, they mounted a vast survey to ascertain the nature of core-raw ESP and to try to develop its natural characteristics. They also recruited individuals with manifest higher-stage talents.

At first, this news was looked upon by American analysts with disbelief, and then amazement. The initial assumption was that it was a campaign of Soviet disinformation, designed to befuddle the West. But after confirmatory studies were completed, and rumors about them had appeared in the press, the American bureaucracy responsible for gauging potential threats began creaking into operation.

The new situation was not without its humorous side. Appropriate American bureaucracies are advised by mainstream scientists who themselves draw upon the academic consensus of opinion. Upon matters pertaining to ESP, the consensus was definitely not propitious. No one of any standing in the various sociopolitical organizations that manage science and the academics wished to jeopardize scientific respectability or their careers.

It was soon discovered that, because of the unimportant status granted by mainstream science to American parapsychology, and above all the latter's middle-groundedness, it and the new Soviet discipline—termed psychoenergetics—were not in any way equivalent sciences. The question probably arose: Could the sudden pumping of funds into parapsychology inspire it to flower overnight into an equivalent of the new psychoenergetics? Would parapsychology be able to change its own sociopolitical perspective? In fairness, these questions have yet to be answered.

One can just imagine the nervous consultations that took place within the planning committees to which these unenviable considerations fell. Over them all hung the ominous threat: Would the Soviets make sufficient progress in their new and extremely well-funded psychoenergetics effort actually to develop an applied ESP? They would almost certainly turn it into an espionage tool if they could. Was there an ESP gap? Would America, in the ESP area, be caught with its pants down?

To compound matters, in 1980 it became known that in the People's Republic of China, ESP studies had suddenly emerged among the top Chinese scientific priorities, and were being given serious consideration, presumably along with appropriate government funding, by highly qualified and specialized physicists and psychologists.

Visions and rumors of psychic armies began to circulate. ESP, it was supposed, would soon become a tactical tool for penetrating a nation's most guarded secrets. America, so long possessed by a dominant antipsychic and anti-ESP consensus among its mainstream scientists, indeed would have a problem should this prove true.

If all the reports in the media are to be believed, psychic technology is already being employed in the "psychic wars" between the United States and the Soviet Union, and possibly also by the People's Republic of China. In this "psi race," the United States may well lag behind because of the manner in which materialistic science views the brain and the human ESP talents in general. Scientific modernists *think* themselves rational scientists, and they consider any phenomena that do not fit into their brand of rationalism to be nonrational—that is, figments of the imagination. If the United States, under the official guidance of the modernist scientific establishment, undertakes extensive ESP research, all attempts to "explain" ESP will be solely in terms of extremely "rational" brain hemisphere controls. It is a bias that first emanated from the Vienna circle of psychiatrists in the early decades of this century, the result of dogmas rejecting psychic principles and seeking the answers to all psychological questions in the *mechanics* of the brain. The general scientific overview of United States programs is based upon these dogmas, as are most of the sterile laboratory methods of psychical research in the United States.

As has been pointed out, if the United States needs to develop psychic abilities like telepathy, precognition, and remote viewing for military intelligence gathering, then it will have to adopt appropriate methods in order to understand the actual basics of psi.

Neither the Soviet Union nor the People's Republic of China is trapped within the constraints of scientific, rational modernism. The general outlook of the People's Republic of China rests upon an ancient philosophical base. Chinese philosophy has always incorporated as realities those aspects of consciousness and human talents that are branded nonrational in the West. The Soviets have exhibited the intensely developed ability to look at all aspects of phenomena, whether regarded irrational by the West or not.

In fact, it appears that the Soviets have used effective approaches to the puzzles of ESP and have already achieved significant results in the "psychic wars race."

Nevertheless, the combined activities of these three powers will certainly serve to raise ESP to a status it has not heretofore enjoyed. This implies that native extrasensory abilities in the not too distant future will be looked on as a resource, much as are intelligence and higher education.

Its coming has been foreshadowed in science fiction; and facts about it have been brought to light by organized research—first called "psychical research," then "parapsychology," and now "psychoenergetics."

Don't let these terms confuse you. They all mean essentially the same thing, and all assume the presence of natural extrasensory perception. Almost everyone has this talent to some degree.

Only those individuals who have made some effort to locate their own raw-core extrasensory capabilities will be in a position to appreciate the age of applied ESP that is now dawning, and perhaps, to be a part of it. One's familiarity with real ESP potential is going to become— indeed it already has—a basis for comprehending applied ESP. Those who do not make an effort to locate their own core ESP will become mere bystanders, unable either to appreciate or take part in the ESP Age now nearly upon us.

Extrasensory perception (external sensing), as well as all psi in general, is caught up in three major myths that feed on each other.

First, at the grass roots level, there exists the myth that ESP experiences are unexplainable. Second, in the parapsychology metastructure, the myth exists that ESP is elusive. Third, in the skeptical superstructures, the myth exists that ESP does not exist and any claims to it are illusory. This myth then feeds back into the experiential grass roots level and keeps ESP *unexplained*, even though over 10 percent of the people continue to experience ESP events.

All this functions as a sort of round robin exercise in which the higher metastructures that are expected to inquire into new things have refused to take upon themselves this onerous burden, because in doing so the very labels that govern the metastructures are in danger of radical change. These metastructures will remain resistant until they are pressured into change by new realities emerging at the grass roots level.

There are several reasons for developing ESP at the individual level, at the grass roots intuitive level. Mainly because any reality established at those levels serves to bring change into the metastructures above them.

It is a bitter truth that the metastructures often become chauvinistic and partisan to their own goals. Some become quite elitist, creating myths of themselves, and then introverting into the myths and living within them.

Every society needs metastructures—or at least has them, whether it wants them or not. One of the greater drawbacks about metastructures is that the higher one goes in them, the less and less allowable unique experiences become. At the top of any given metastructure, the only allowable experiences are those that personify the dogmas upon which the cutting edge of the metastructure is being sharpened. Often this cutting edge is quite dull, formed only out of what was respectable in the past.

The individual at the grass roots level has the widest possible experiencing opportunities. It is at this level that we find the largest and most powerful ESP experiences.

The statistics we have are not all that indicative. It appears that at least 10 percent of the population will experience some life-changing ESP event in their lives, while upwards of 80 percent believe in the existence of ESP. This is the level in which raw-core ESP functions spontaneously. At the top of many metastructures where ESP is a forbidden topic, very little ESP surfaces, or at least it is not admitted to.

In one of his exhaustive books, *Science and Parascience*, veteran writer Brian Inglis puts his finger neatly on the basic issues involved:

> Some skeptics are prepared to concede that the quantity of evidence is impressive; but this, they claim, is irrelevant because there is no single totally convincing case. . . . The disturbing fact is that the academic world is still in the grip of the materialist faith which Tyndall preached, in spite of the way in which the quantum physicists have undermined its foundations. . . . Quantum physics has continued to provide evidence of paranormal-type phenomena, translocation and action-at-a-distance, at the micro level, and Bergson, Geley and others made a start in explaining why and how the phenomena take the form they do at the macro level. . . . The main problem here is that whereas the new physics could replace the old without disturbing anybody except physicists, to accept the reality of the paranormal phenomena would mean making nonsense of much that is still being taken for granted, and taught, in many other disciplines: in biology, psychology, anthropology, medicine and even history; most of all, perhaps, in philosophy.*

*Brian Inglis, *Science and Parascience*, Hodder and Stoughton, London, 1984, pp. 338–339.

The principal phenomenon of the seventies and the eighties is the emergence of what is being called New Age thought. It is a grass roots movement, forming in protest of the inadequacies of the higher superstructures to envision a new holistic life system. The overall goal of the New Age is to restore a visionary element in society, one that allows social energies to see beyond the myths that have entrapped the superstructures in policies that are now threatening the entire human biosphere and the world's ecosphere. Unless these myths are broken down, there's going to be hell to pay.

The New Age method of trying to attack this problem is to experience illumination at the individual level. As author Marilyn Ferguson so aptly put it: "Let there be change, and let it begin within myself."

ESP/external sensing has a great role to play in this transformation. Even the smallest experience of one's own ability to be aware of human elements that transcend the boundaries of the physical body can serve to link up holistic consciousness in a way never before envisioned. Rather than merely seeking to demonstrate the reality of ESP in a parapsychological laboratory, it is of much greater importance that individuals be able to experience ESP personally, however minimally. At this level, the reality of ESP will be much greater and more valuable than at the top of the superstructures where any ESP phenomenon tends to be regarded as only a curiosity.

It has been my finding that ESP, once experienced, reinforces the concept of the interconnectedness of all humanity, all life. The shortest and surest way of enlarging this reality is through experiencing hard-wired ESP, because through it the individual can confirm the accuracy of ESP, and the existence within himself of an ESP core. There is, of course, a great well of ESP beyond hard-wire examples. But once one has achieved a notable example of it, then the existence of human ESP becomes self-evident with all that it implies.

Beneath this obviously greater issue are other reasons why ESP should be contacted and developed in a new frame of reference.

At the personal level, highly developed ESP can be potentially very beneficial. There are many practical applications for ESP. Some developed psychics have been very good at them. Telepathic contact with family or loved ones, especially when they are troubled, has frequently been reported. ESP is sometimes helpful in finding lost objects and other people. It is nice to be able to read another's thoughts and to intuit inventions and philosophical insights. "Seeing" through walls, identifying face-down playing cards at the gambling table, selecting winners at the races or in the lottery, and penetrating the secrets of the stock market are far less successful, but some developed psychics have been able to do so at times.

All human talents possess a core—an embryo—which can grow and develop. The growth and development are the result of precision, training, practice, and intuitive understanding.

A good example is the revolution that has taken place in sports. At one time, only the building of endurance through forced practice was emphasized. Today, a desire to perfect performance through understanding the whole organism has developed a holistic way of looking at the athlete. Proper nourishment, sleep cycles, vitamin reinforcement, understanding, reducing overtraining, short-cycle training, and so on, are now all included in sports practice. This attitude has also been adopted by many in the performing arts, the intellectual arts, and even in the military and the martial arts.

Within each of these various talents, a core can be identified. From this embryonic stage the rudimentary talent can be identified, understood, and developed. Failure to develop the talent may cause it to recede or disappear altogether.

Bearing all this in mind, we can perhaps see that what

is needed is a more holistic approach to the basic and raw-core ESP phenomena.

Knowledge and raw experience must precede training and practice to make it precise and effective. One cannot become effectively psychic by will alone any more than a pole vaulter can surpass the eighteen-foot mark by willing it. This is understood and accepted in sports, but not yet in parapsychology.

Eventually, it will become understood. All the evidence points to the fact that in the Soviet Union holistic development of athletes is far superior to similar work in the rest of the world. The evidence also suggests that in Russia, psychic development is already on a holistic platform. It is this and only this—seen as a potential threat by American analysts—that has inspired a new interest in ESP and psi at the governmental level.

The realities of ESP should not be permitted to remain clouded in the upper reaches of the metastructures which tend to conduct themselves based in old realities. The extrasensory experience is, after all, experienced by people. The true guide and the guiding principles can only come from the grass roots, which trusts experience more than it does intellectual ideas.

So it is you who must be willing to experience ESP, and guide its development into those more spiritual directions that ESP itself is a part of.

Only then will the real significance and the true and valuable future of ESP be seen and understood.

△ SELECTED BIBLIOGRAPHY △

Historical Picture Drawing Sources

George Albert Smith: *Proceedings of the Society for Psychical Research*, April 1883, Vol. 1, Part II; and Vol. 1, Part III.

Miss Edwards and Miss Relph: *Proceedings of the Society for Psychical Research*, April 1884, Part V.

Miss Kate Smith: *Proceedings of the Society for Psychical Research*, July 1884, Part VI.

The Schmoll Experiments: *Proceedings of the Society for Psychical Research*, June 1888, Part XII.

The Max Dessoir Experiments: *Proceedings of the Society for Psychical Research*, December 1888, Part XIII.

The Schrenck-Notzing Experiments: *Proceedings of the Society for Psychical Research*, April 1891, Part XVIII.

The Warcollier Experiments: *Journal of the American Society for Psychical Research*, December 1939, Vol. XXXII, No. 12.

René Warcollier, *Mind to Mind*, Creative Age Press, New York, 1948.

The Upton Sinclair Experiments: Upton Sinclair, *Mental Radio*, Werner Laurie, London, 1930, reprinted 1951.

The SRI International Experiments: Private publications.

The ASPR Experiments: Private holdings of the author.

Arnheim, Rudolf, *Art and Visual Perception*, University of California Press, Berkeley and Los Angeles, 1974.

Ashby, R. H., *The Guidebook for the Study of Psychical Research*, Rider, London, 1972.

Beloff, J., "Is Normal Memory a 'Paranormal' Phenomenon?," *Theory to Theory*, Vol. 14, 1980.

Bohm, David, "The Implicate Order: A New Order for Physics," *Process Studies*, Vol. 8, 1978.

————, *Wholeness and the Implicate Order*, Routledge & Kegan Paul, London and Boston, 1980.

Capra, Fritjof, *The Tao of Physics: An Exploration of the Parallels between Modern Physics and Eastern Mysticism*, Bantam Books, New York, 1977.

Davies, P. C. W., *The Physics of Time Asymmetry*, University of California Press, Berkeley, 1977.

Denton, J. Snider, *Feeling Psychologically Treated*, Sigma Publishing Co., St. Louis, 1905.

Dingwall, Eric J., *Abnormal Hypnotic Phenomena* (five vols.), J. & A. Churchill Ltd., London, 1967.

Dixon, N. F., *Subliminal Perception*, McGraw-Hill, London, 1971.

————, *Preconscious Processing*, John Wiley & Sons, New York, 1981.

Dubrov, A. P., and V. N. Pushkin, *Parapsychology and Contemporary Science*, Consultants Bureau, New York, 1982.

Ebon, Martin, *Psychic Warfare*, McGraw-Hill, New York, 1983.

Edwards, Betty, *Drawing on the Artist Within*, Simon and Schuster, New York, 1986.

————, *Drawing on the Right Side of the Brain*, J. P. Tarcher, Los Angeles, 1979.

Ehrenwald, Jan, *The ESP Experience*, Basic Books, New York, 1978.

Ferguson, Marilyn, *The Brain Revolution: The Frontiers of Mind Research*, Taplinger Publishing Co., New York, 1973.

————, *The Aquarian Conspiracy*, J. P. Tarcher, 1980.

Gablik, Suzi, "Changing Paradigms," in *New Art Examiner*, June 1985.

Gauld, Alan, *The Founders of Psychical Research*, Routledge & Kegan Paul, London, 1968.

Goldberg, Philip, *The Intuitive Edge*, J. P. Tarcher, Los Angeles, 1983.

Hall, Trevor H., *The Strange Case of Edmund Gurney*, Gerald Duckworth & Co. Ltd., London, 1964.

Hayles, N. Katherine, *The Cosmic Web*, Cornell University Press, Ithaca, N.Y., and London, 1984.

Haynes, Renee, *The Society for Psychical Research, 1882–1982, A History*, MacDonald & Co., London, 1982.

Hettinger, J., *Exploring the Ultra-Perceptive Facility*, Rider & Co., London, 1941.

Hinkle, L.E., Jr., "The physiological state of the interrogation subject as it affects brain function," in *The Manipulation of Human Behaviour*, Albert B. Biderman and Herbert Zimmer (eds), John Wiley & Sons, New York, 1961.

Inglis, Brian, *Natural and Supernatural*, Hodder and Stoughton, London, 1984.

————, *Science and Parascience*, a history of the paranormal, 1914–1939, Hodder and Stoughton, London, 1984.

Mackie, J. L., *The Cement of the Universe*, Oxford University Press, Oxford, 1984.

Mauskopf, Seymour H., and Michael R. McVaugh, *The Elusive Science*, Johns Hopkins University Press, Baltimore, 1980.

Osty, Eugene, *Supernormal Faculties in Man*, Methuen & Co. Ltd., London, 1923.

Prince, Walter Franklin, *Noted Witnesses for Psychic Occurrences*, University Books, New Hyde Park, N.Y., 1963.

Puthoff, H. E., and R. Targ, "A Perceptual Channel for Information Transfer over Kilometer Distances: Historical Perspective and Recent Research," *Proceedings of the IEEE*, LXIV, March 1976.

Schmeidler, Gertrude (ed), *Extrasensory Perception*, Atherton Press, New York, 1969.

Sheldrake, Rupert, *A New Science of Life*, J. P. Tarcher, Los Angeles, 1981.

Soal, S. G., and H. T. Bowden, *The Mind Readers*, Doubleday, Garden City, N.Y., 1960.

Talamonti, Leo, *Forbidden Universe: Mysteries of the Psychic World*, Stein and Day, New York, 1974.

Targ, R., and H. E. Puthoff, "Information Transmission under Conditions of Sensory Shielding," *Nature*, CCLI, October 1974.

————, *Mind-Reach*, Delacorte Press/Eleanor Friede, New York, 1977.

Vasiliev, L. L., *Experiments in Distant Influence*, E.P. Dutton, New York, 1976.

Wilkins, Sir Hubert, and Harold M. Sherman, *Thoughts through Space*, Fawcett Publications, Greenwich, Conn., 1973.

Wilson, Ian, *All in the Mind*, Doubleday, Garden City, N.Y., 1982.

Wolf, Fred Alan, *Star Wave: Mind, Consciousness, and Quantum Physics*, Macmillan, New York, 1984.

△ INDEX △